"Adrian Rogers is one of the greatest preachers of our age, a man of tremendous conviction and deep biblical insight. God has used him in a remarkable way, and Adrian Rogers speaks with the voice of dedicated experience and biblical authority. *The Passion of Christ and the Purpose of Life* is his most important book yet. This is a powerful defense of the Gospel, and a masterful presentation of the substitutionary nature of Christ's atonement. Dr. Rogers hits the critical issues with full force, and takes his readers into some of the deepest questions about God's saving work in Christ. All believers will benefit by considering his arguments and seeking the mind of Christ. This faithful pastor is passionate about the meaning of Christ's passion—and about the Gospel that so powerfully saves."

> R. ALBERT MOHLER, JR., President
> The Southern Baptist Theological Seminary

"Adrian Rogers, the quintessential pastoral preacher, is delivering his heart to his people at Bellevue Baptist Church in Memphis, Tennessee. This is vintage Rogers. His handling of the extent of the atonement of Christ is alone worth the price of the book many times over."

> PAIGE PATTERSON, President, Southwestern Baptist
> Theological Seminary, Fort Worth, Texas

"Dr. Adrian Rogers beautifully sets forth the glories of the sufferings of our Lord as they apply to life's purpose. Read this book to be blessed and to be challenged."

> JERRY VINES, Pastor, First Baptist Church,
> Jacksonville, Florida

"I have known Dr. Adrian Rogers for many years now, and have come to love him like a brother. I have deep respect and admiration for his unwavering commitment to the cause of Christ and have benefited immensely from his godly wisdom and discernment."

> JAMES DOBSON, Focus on the Family

D1206755

The Passion of Christ and the Purpose of Life

The
PASSION OF CHRIST
and the
PURPOSE OF LIFE

ADRIAN ROGERS

CROSSWAY BOOKS

A MINISTRY OF
GOOD NEWS PUBLISHERS
WHEATON, ILLINOIS

The Passion of Christ and the Purpose of Life

Copyright © 2005 by Adrian Rogers

Published by Crossway Books
    A ministry of Good News Publishers
    1300 Crescent Street
    Wheaton, Illinois 60187

All rights reserved. No part of this publication may be reproduced, stored in a retrieval system or transmitted in any form by any means, electronic, mechanical, photocopy, recording or otherwise, without the prior permission of the publisher, except as provided by USA copyright law.

Cover design: Josh Dennis

First printing, 2005

Printed in the United States of America

Unless otherwise indicated, all Scripture quotations are taken from the King James Version.

Library of Congress Cataloging-in-Publication Data
Rogers, Adrian.
   The passion of Christ and the purpose of life / Adrian Rogers.
     p. cm.
   ISBN 1-58134-651-4
   1. Jesus Christ—Crucifixion—Meditations. 2. Jesus Christ—Passion—Meditations. 3. Christian life. I. Title
BT453.R64   2005
232.96—dc22   2004029335

DP		13	12	11	10	09	08	07	06	05
15	14	13	12	11	10	9	8	7	6	5	4	3	2	1

CONTENTS

ACKNOWLEDGMENTS

I want to thank the people whose support, encouragement, and faithful work helped make this book possible: the staff at Love Worth Finding Ministries; Linda Glance, my faithful secretary; President Lane Dennis, Vice President Marvin Padgett, Managing Editor Ted Griffin, and all the helpful people at Crossway Books; and my editor and friend, Philip Rawley. You are all the greatest and dear friends.

Also, I wish to acknowledge the membership of the dear church that received these messages with open hearts and minds. What an encouragement they continue to be to me.

INTRODUCTION

When actor Mel Gibson's film *The Passion of the Christ* finally debuted in theaters across America in February 2004, it arrived amid more media hype, audience anticipation, and bitter controversy than probably any film in the previous half century.

You may recall that the publicity, and the public debate, about this film started many months before it was released. Critics scorned, denounced, and dismissed the work as a piece of narrow-minded, religious propaganda. Many Christians waited with great excitement as they learned of Gibson's plan to use only the Gospel accounts of Jesus' crucifixion for the film's story line and dialogue.

In the middle of all this, I rejoiced to know that *The Passion of the Christ* caused millions of people to think about and talk about the cross of Jesus Christ and why He died. Some of the biggest names in the entertainment and religious worlds appeared on prime-time television programs to discuss questions such as: Why did Jesus die? Who really crucified Jesus? What was the real purpose for which He died?

I believe Mel Gibson has done the church a service by shining the light on Jesus' crucifixion and helping people understand it in a way they never had before. The questions his film raised in the popular mind are the most important questions any person could ever ask—not just in our day, but in any day. This book is dedicated to helping answer questions like these, and to lifting the passion of our Lord Jesus Christ off the pages of Scripture and into your heart. My prayer throughout these studies was that God would draw me to the foot of the cross, and now that is my prayer for you, dear reader.

PART I

CRUCIAL QUESTIONS ABOUT CHRIST'S PASSION

1

WHY DID JESUS HAVE TO DIE?

One of the saddest and most perplexing stories to come out of World War II was the case of Private Eddie Slovik, the only American soldier executed for desertion during that long war.

Private Slovik had come from a very troubled and difficult background and seemed to be just getting his life together when he received his army draft notice. He completed his training and was shipped off to Europe. But his first experience of combat so terrified him that he laid down his weapon and refused to return to his unit. Although he knew that the sentence for desertion in time of war was death by firing squad, Private Slovik did not believe he would really be executed.

But as the case moved through the military justice system, it became more and more obvious not only that Private Slovik had deserted, but that the law was clear on his punishment. Even though no one involved with the case was eager to carry out his duty, Eddie Slovik was eventually executed for desertion. The details of the case were kept under such wraps that Private Slovik's widow did not learn until some years later that her husband had actually died at the hands of a U.S. military firing squad rather than in combat.

For many people, the Eddie Slovik case raised the difficult question, did this young man really have to die? That question cannot be answered with finality or to everyone's satisfaction. But in the case of another young Man in the prime of His life, we can say on the authority of God's Word that Jesus Christ had to die. This does not mean that Jesus had no choice about the matter. It was His mighty love that made any other choice unthinkable. In this opening chapter I want to address the all-important issue of *why* Jesus had to die.

Some of those who debated *The Passion of the Christ* argued vociferously that Jesus was nothing more than a religious martyr who died for what He believed. Others said He died as an example to show us how to die with grace and dignity. Still other people believe that Jesus' death was simply a first-century miscarriage of justice in which an innocent man died tragically at the hands of His enemies.

Seven hundred years before Jesus walked the shores of Galilee, the prophet Isaiah dipped his pen in golden glory and wrote some amazing words that still affect us in the twenty-first century:

> *Surely he hath borne our griefs, and carried our sorrows: yet we did esteem him stricken, smitten of God, and afflicted. But he was wounded for our transgressions, he was bruised for our iniquities: the chastisement of our peace was upon him; and with his stripes we are healed. All we like sheep have gone astray; we have turned every one to his own way; and the* LORD *hath laid on him the iniquity of us all. (Isaiah 53:4-6)*

Now let's look at 1 Peter 3:18 and read the words of the apostle that shed the light of heaven on Isaiah's prophecy: "For Christ also hath once suffered for sins, the just for the unjust, that he might bring us to God." This wonderful verse is packed with gospel dynamite, which I want to unpack one stick of truth at a time. Here in one brief statement is God's answer as to why Jesus died.

Make no mistake about it. Even though the cross was far more than just a human tragedy, it *was* tragic. In fact, the greatest tragedy and the greatest injustice the world has ever known took place on a barren hill just outside the city of Jerusalem, where the Son of God hung in bloody agony upon a cross with darkness veiling His glowing face. There was an earthquake: The ground trembled, and the rocks split open as Satan and the dark forces of hell battered against the very gates of glory.

But to find out why Jesus died, we have to look beyond the evils perpetrated on Jesus by sinful men and hateful demons. For the greater truth is that it pleased God the Father to send His sinless, precious, only Son to the cross. We are going to see that Calvary was not only the earth's greatest tragedy—it was also God's greatest triumph. God had a purpose for His Son's death, a purpose so deep and so great that your destiny and mine are wrapped up in it. Consider at least four reasons Peter gave in 1 Peter 3:18 in answer to the question, why did Jesus have to die?

THE SUBSTITUTIONARY PURPOSE OF THE CROSS

The first thing you need to understand about Jesus' death is that He died *in our place*, as our substitute. The Bible says Jesus died as "the just for the unjust."

Jesus was the just one, completely innocent of any sin. But He went to the cross and died for us who had already been tried and convicted of sin in heaven's courtroom. Jesus Christ did not die as a helpless victim. He said, "No man taketh [my life] from me, but I lay it down of myself. I have power to lay it down, and

I have power to take it again" (John 10:18). On the cross, Jesus took the death stroke for sin that we deserved.

God Cannot Simply Overlook Our Sin

Here is the heart of the matter of why Jesus had to die. When the Bible says that God is just, it means that He is perfectly, totally, and completely righteous, holy, and separated from sin. And being just, God cannot overlook sin. The Bible says that God "will not at all acquit the wicked" (Nahum 1:3).

If you were to go through all of the dictionaries in the world to find one word that would describe God, what do you think that word would be? Most people would say it is the word *love*, because the Bible says in 1 John 4:8, "God is love." But if you had to find one word that more than any other captured the essence of God's nature, it would be the word *holy*. "Holy, holy, holy, is the LORD of hosts," the seraphim cry ceaselessly in heaven (Isaiah 6:3).

God's holiness means that He is the complete antithesis of sin. God's holiness burns against sin. His holiness regards sin as a clenched fist in His face. Sin is a repudiation of all that God is.

We Are Full of Sin

But if you were to search all the dictionaries and lexicons for a word that best describes mankind, it would be the word *sinful*. "For all have sinned, and come short of the glory of God" (Romans 3:23). There is a chasm as wide as eternity between a holy, sinless God and sinful man. The glory of God is His holiness. The shame of mankind is our sin.

That's why the world doesn't like to talk about sin. The world says man may be weak, but he's not wicked. He may be flawed, but he's not depraved. Pick up the newspaper tomorrow, and you will read about murder, rape, corporate scandals, child abuse, and a myriad of other terrible things. But I doubt that you will find the word *sin* used even one time.

Merely ignoring our sin doesn't get rid of it, however. So we have a problem, which is that God is holy and just and must judge sin, and yet we are filled with sin. Now God has a problem too, if I can say that respectfully. The problem is that this holy God who must punish sin also loves us sinners and is "not willing that any should perish" (2 Peter 3:9). So how can He punish sin and love the sinner at the same time?

Someone might say, "Well, can't God just overlook sin? He can do anything He wants to do, and since He loves sinners and wants them to be saved, why doesn't He just say, 'I forgive you,' without requiring that sin be punished?"

The reason is that simply overlooking sin would not make God loving, but only unjust and unfair. I doubt if any victim of a heinous crime would be satisfied to have the judge say to the criminal, "I'm basically a loving person. So I am going to overlook what you did and let you go." They say in a court of law that when a guilty man is acquitted, the judge is condemned. A judge who acquits the guilty cannot justify his actions by claiming that it was an act of love.

Of course, comparisons between human justice and God's righteous judgment eventually break down, because His justice is flawless. Not so in our world. A missionary who ministers in a large men's prison in an African country was told recently by the prison administrator that at least 70 percent of the men in that prison are actually innocent of the crimes for which they were convicted.

This official explained that the real criminals got away, while these men just happened to be in the wrong place at the wrong time. The police needed someone to arrest; so the accused were taken. And since they do not have the money to pay off the officials, they are suffering while the guilty go unpunished.

If God allowed sin to go unpunished, He would violate His nature and topple from His throne of holiness. He would break His law that says, "The wages of sin is death," and "The soul that sinneth, it shall die" (Romans 6:23; Ezekiel 18:4). God cannot violate His holiness and overlook sin.

The Cross Is God's Eternal Provision for Our Sin

But because God is a God of infinite love, the Father, Son, and Holy Spirit drew up a plan in the councils of eternity past that called for God the Son to take our sin upon Himself and go to the cross. The cross was not an accident or an afterthought but was in the heart and mind of God from all eternity. The Bible calls Jesus "the Lamb slain before the foundation of the world" (Revelation 13:8).

Before God framed this universe, before He flung out the sun, moon, and stars, scooped out the oceans, and heaped up the mountains, before you and I were ever born, God saw the cross. His eternal decree is that "without shedding of blood is no remission" for sin (Hebrews 9:22). That is why Jesus Christ was born in the shadow of the cross.

The cross is pictured, prophesied, and portrayed from the book of Genesis to the book of Revelation. In a sense the river of blood that flowed from Jesus' side on the cross began in a figure flowing in the Garden of Eden. When Adam and Eve sinned and tried to hide their shame with fig leaves, God clothed them with garments made of animal skins (Genesis 3:21). You cannot make an animal-skin garment without killing the animal. God was teaching us that the guilt of sin must be dealt with by the shedding of blood.

Then in Genesis 4:1-5 we read that Adam's two sons, Cain and Abel, brought their offerings to the Lord. Abel was a shepherd who brought God a blood sacrifice by killing a lamb from his flock. But Cain was a farmer who tried to offer God fruits and vegetables from the ground that God had cursed because of sin. God accepted Abel's offering but rejected Cain's. Why? Because without the shedding of blood, there is no remission for sin.

Then God destroyed the world with a flood and saved Noah and seven others with him. When they came out of the ark, the first thing Noah did was to offer a blood sacrifice upon an altar (Genesis 8:20). Why? Because without the shedding of blood, there is no remission for sin.

That river of blood next surfaced in the life of Abraham, the first Hebrew, as God called him out of paganism to Canaan (Genesis 12:1-3). God promised Abraham a son even though he was too old to have children and Sarah's womb was dead. But God gave Abraham a miracle son, Isaac.

But when Isaac was a young, strapping boy, God said to Abraham, "Take now thy son, thine only son Isaac, whom thou lovest . . . and offer him there for a burnt offering upon one of the mountains which I will tell thee of" (Genesis 22:2). Abraham must have been in agony, but he knew that if God wanted him to sacrifice Isaac, He could raise him from the dead.

So Abraham went to Mount Moriah, the place that would later be known as Mount Calvary, prepared an altar, and laid Isaac on it. But as Abraham took the knife to slay his son, God stayed his hand. Abraham looked up and saw a ram—crowned with thorns, if you will—caught in a thicket. God provided a substitute for Isaac, because blood had to be shed for the remission of sin.

And then this red river of blood flowed into Egypt, where the people of Abraham were formed into a nation in the midst of their slavery. When God got ready to deliver Israel from Egypt, the first thing He did was to command the people to sacrifice a lamb and put its blood on the doorposts of their homes so that when God's death angel came, he would "pass over" the Israelites. God told Moses, "When I see the blood, I will pass over you" (Exodus 12:1-13).

The Jews were also instructed to eat their lambs in a meal that came to be known as the Passover feast. An innocent lamb was killed as a substitute for the people in each Jewish home, and its blood was posted. If the Israelites had put diamonds or rubies on their doorposts, that would have done no good. Had they put up poetry and sentiment rather than sacrifice, that would have done no good. Neither would it have done any good to take a spotless lamb and tie it alive to their doorposts. God was cleansing His people, but that required blood.

This red river of blood continued to flow throughout the Bible until one day it reached its climax in the Lord Jesus Christ. John the Baptist pointed to Jesus one day and cried, "Behold the Lamb of God, which taketh away the sin of the world" (John 1:29).

The Shadow of the Cross Fell upon Jesus

Hebrews 10:1 tells us that all of those Old Testament sacrifices were only a "shadow" of the reality to come. A shadow is only an outline that has no detail or color. It's not the shadow that really matters, but the reality it represents. The Old Testament's sacrifices were just getting people ready for Jesus to come. God was teaching us that the wages of sin is death, and that nothing but shed blood can atone for sin. Sin always brings death in God's holy court of justice.

Now we can begin to see why Peter said that Jesus died in our place, "the just for the unjust" (1 Peter 3:18). The Lord Jesus hung His head on the cross and died on the same limestone ridge where so long before Abraham had found God's substitute sacrifice in a thicket, and where the priests were the very day of

Jesus' death putting to death innocent lambs on the Passover. This is the substitutionary purpose of the cross.

THE SUFFERING PASSION OF THE CROSS

Notice also that 1 Peter 3:18 says Jesus "suffered" on the cross. Here is the second reason Jesus had to die. Sin brings suffering as surely as night follows day, and God's holiness demands that someone must suffer for sin. But because of His magnificent grace, it pleased God to let the suffering we deserved fall upon His Son. The agony Jesus endured in Gethsemane, in His beatings, and on the cross is what is meant by the passion of the Christ. Think of all the suffering Jesus Christ endured to be our Substitute.

Christ Suffered Emotional Agony in Gethsemane

The cross was still hours away when Jesus arrived at Gethsemane with His disciples. Luke records, "And when he was at the place he said unto them, Pray that ye enter not into temptation. And he was withdrawn from them about a stone's cast, and kneeled down, and prayed" (Luke 22:40-41).

The word *Gethsemane* means "olive press," the place where olives were crushed under intense pressure to extract their oil. This name speaks symbolically of the extreme emotional pressure Jesus was feeling as He left the Upper Room and walked across Jerusalem. He and the disciples went down into the Kidron Valley to reach the Mount of Olives.

Bible scholars tell us that the brook at Kidron was most likely flowing red with blood when Jesus crossed it because the blood of literally thousands of Passover sacrifices in Jerusalem was drained there. When Jesus crossed that crimson stream, doubtless it spoke to Him of His own blood that was going to be poured out very soon.

Jesus went to this olive grove and prayed, "Father, if thou be willing, remove this cup from me" (v. 42). Jesus' "cup" was a metaphor for the sufferings He had to drink to the very last drop as our substitute.

What was in that cup that made the Lord Jesus shrink back in dread? The *pollution* of sin was in that cup: "For he [God] hath made him [Jesus] to be sin for us, who knew no sin" (2 Corinthians 5:21). Even though Jesus was the sinless, spotless, stainless Lamb of God, all of the sin of the world was distilled in that cup of suffering that He had to drink for us.

Do you realize what that meant? It meant that blasphemy against God settled in that cup. Rape and adultery and sexual perversion settled in that cup, along with the bitterness of child abuse and wife beating. Hitler's gas ovens were in that cup. The murder of innocent children by abortion was in that cup. Satanic worship was in that cup. Pride, lust, envy, self-righteousness, and every other vile sin you can name were in that cup. And Jesus had to drink all of it.

Not only the pollution of sin, but also the *punishment* of sin was in the cup Jesus drank. The Bible says in Isaiah 53:10, "It pleased the Lord to bruise him." Some translations (for example, the *English Standard Version*) render this, "to crush him." Paul said that God the Father "spared not his own Son" (Romans 8:32). This means God held back nothing when He laid the suffering for our sins upon Christ. Jesus took the full force of the Father's fiery wrath against sin.

No one has ever suffered like Jesus. You may have heard a theologian say that Jesus took the hell we deserve. That is not an overstatement, for in His passion Jesus suffered the eternity in hell that our sins deserve.

But how could Jesus suffer an eternity of hell in a matter of hours? Because He, being infinite, suffered in a finite period of time what we, being finite, would suffer in an infinite period of time. The sins of the world were distilled upon Jesus, and eternity was compressed upon Him.

People who are undergoing intense suffering often say that every second seems like a minute, every minute like an hour, and every hour like a day. Well, every minute of Jesus' suffering was like an eternity. But even this does not do justice to the depth of our Savior's emotional and spiritual suffering.

No wonder He lay prostrate on the ground in Gethsemane (Matthew 26:39), with red blood and black dirt on His face, pleading, "Father, if there be some other way, please let this cup pass from Me." But the silence from heaven said there was no other way. And the dear Savior said, "Thy will be done."

I want to show you one more thing about Jesus' emotional suffering. In Luke 22:44 we read, "Being in an agony he prayed more earnestly." The word *agony* speaks of a contest. In the Greek language, the *agon* was a wrestling match. Jesus was wrestling, not with God the Father or with Satan, but with His own humanity. Jesus did not just stroll to the cross and say, "I am God; so this won't bother Me." His agony was so great in Gethsemane that an angel had to come and strengthen Him so He could go to the cross (Luke 22:43).

Christ Also Suffered Excruciating Physical Pain

It is well documented that crucifixion was one of the most brutal and painful ways to die. But Jesus suffered a beating that would have killed an ordinary man even before He was nailed to that cruel Roman cross.

One of the objections made to Mel Gibson's film was the length of time and the incredible realism given to Jesus' scourging at the hands of the Roman soldiers. I saw the film, and yet I don't believe it portrayed the half of what it was really like.

A Roman scourging was inhumanly brutal. The victim's

hands were tied to a column, and two volunteers—probably psychopaths who volunteered for the job—began to whip the victim with the infamous cat-o'-nine-tails, a sturdy handle with leather thongs that had bits of bone, glass, and lead that would tear away the victim's flesh.

By the time a scourging was over, the victim's body was laid bare. These soldiers knew how to administer the beating to bring a person to the point of death without actually killing him. This is what Jesus endured, not to mention the other torture described in the Gospels in which soldiers punched Him in the face, beat Him with bamboo clubs, and pressed a crown of thorns on His head. Only when all of this was over was Jesus forced to carry the heavy crossbeam to His crucifixion.

I will spare you the gruesome description of a Roman crucifixion, except to say that every detail was designed to produce maximum pain and to prolong the person's death. Jesus' nails were put through nerves to cause fiery pain to shoot through His body, and His knees were bent so He would slump down and begin to suffocate. The only way to breathe was to push up with one's legs on those nailed feet, which was why the soldiers broke the legs of the two thieves who were crucified with Jesus, so they would suffocate (John 19:32).

A Major League baseball player who was speaking to a Christian group told about a church he visited where they had a full-sized model of the cross. People were invited to get on the cross and assume a position like that in which Jesus hung. This ballplayer, a strong man in superb condition, wanted to try it. But he said he could not stand the searing pain in his shoulders for more than a few seconds without having to get off. As a believer, he then testified to his utter amazement at the suffering Jesus must have endured.

The cross was, by definition, excruciating pain. Did you know that the Latin word *excrutiatus*, from which we get our

English word *excruciating*, means "out of the cross"? This word was coined to describe the worst kind of pain, which Jesus suffered in our place because someone has to suffer to fulfill God's righteous penalty against sin. Jesus' agony should bring tears to our eyes and sorrow to our hearts. To think that One so perfect and innocent suffered for our sins.

THE SETTLED PROVISION OF THE CROSS

A third reason Jesus had to die is that sin demands full payment to the offended holiness of God. Jesus suffered and died to pay for sin. But hallelujah, He had to suffer only once! In 1 Peter 3:18 we find this declaration: "Christ also hath *once* suffered for sins" (emphasis added). Peter had heard Jesus say so on the cross when He cried out, "It is finished" (John 19:30), before He bowed His head and dismissed His spirit.

The phrase Jesus uttered is one magnificent word in Greek, *tetelestai*, which means "paid in full." In Jesus' day when a man was put in prison, a certificate of debt would be nailed to his prison door stating his crime and the penalty. When the prisoner had served his time, the judge would write across this certificate, "Paid in full," and give it to the man so he could never be punished again for the same crime. If anyone ever accused him again, the former felon could produce his certificate and say, "You can't touch me. My debt has been paid."

What debt did Jesus pay in full on the cross? Your sin-debt and mine. So when the devil comes to taunt and accuse you for your sins, you can point to God's Word and say, "You can't touch me because this is my bill of deliverance. The debt for my sin has been paid by Jesus on the cross once and for all."

If you know Christ as your Savior, "Paid in full" is written in crimson red over your sin-debt in the records of heaven's court!

THE SAVING POWER OF THE CROSS

Here is the fourth and final reason Peter gave for the death of Jesus: "Christ also hath once suffered for sins, the just for the unjust, *that he might bring us to God*" (emphasis added). The Greek word translated "bring" was often used when a person was brought into the throne room to see a king.

I have had the privilege of being invited to the Oval Office in the White House, and I can tell you this much—you do not stroll into that place without proper clearance or without supervision. Someone will meet you and escort you into this room that is the closest thing to a throne room in America.

No one will just stroll into heaven either. When you and I come into heaven's throne room, there is One who will take us by the hand and bring us in. His name is Jesus. He can bring us to God by the saving power of the blood He shed on the cross. "Nothing but the blood" will get anyone into God's heaven.

A man once imagined himself dying and waiting to get into heaven. As he waited, another man came and knocked on heaven's door. The voice within said, "Who is it that seeks entrance into heaven, and on what basis?"

The man said, "I'm a moral man, and I expect to be admitted based on my honesty in life."

But the voice within heaven said, "Depart from me, you worker of iniquity. I never knew you."

Another man knocked on heaven's door and was asked the same question. He replied, "I am a humanitarian, and I have practiced charity toward the poor."

But the voice on the inside of heaven's door said, "Depart from me, you worker of iniquity. I never knew you."

Then a third man knocked, and in response to the question he said, "I am a religious man who has been faithful in church attendance. I have been baptized, gave my offerings, and followed all the rituals of my religion."

But a third time the voice said, "Depart from me, you worker of iniquity. I never knew you."

A fourth man who knocked on heaven's door gave this answer to the question: "In my hand no price I bring, simply to Christ's cross I cling."

The voice within said, "Open wide the gates and let him in, for of such is the kingdom of heaven." The cross of Christ has saving power for all who will receive Him and put their faith in Him alone for salvation. Jesus will take these by the hand and bring them to God.

Jesus had to die if we were to be delivered from the eternal hell our sins deserved. The agony and pain were all His, and the blessings are all ours. Hallelujah, what a Savior!

2

WHO CRUCIFIED JESUS?

O f all the controversy stirred up by the release of the film *The Passion of the Christ*, perhaps the biggest firestorm was created by the question that is the title of this chapter. Many leaders in the Jewish community reacted angrily, saying the film would inflame anti-Semitism by bringing up the charge that the Jews killed Jesus and are guilty of His blood.

Actor Mel Gibson defended his work, saying that it was not his intention to stir up ill feelings or make accusations against Jews. He simply wanted to tell the story of Jesus' crucifixion as the Bible tells it. This debate planted the cross squarely in the center of America's public consciousness for months on end, and I believe the film helped move the church from cultural Christianity, with its cult of conformity and comfort, back to the vital aspects of the cross and what it means. Would to God we could learn anew the truth of Paul's declaration, "God forbid that I should glory, save in the cross of our Lord Jesus Christ" (Galatians 6:14).

The cross is more than a beautiful ornament to wear around your neck or an insignia at the top of a church steeple. The cross is the turning point of all history. The cross is God's testimony to the sinfulness of human nature. The cross is the mightiest demonstration of the unfathomable love of God. And the cross is the only hope for a dying and rotting society.

Some people, even in the church, complain that we should not focus on the cross because it was so bloody and brutal. You'll recall that many reviewers of Gibson's film objected to the bloody detail and the length of the scenes of Jesus' torture and death. But if anything, the film understated the case. Jesus suffered hours of beatings and mockings and then hung on the cross for six more hours.

Jesus' death was cruel and violent, and what makes it even more brutal was the fact that every blow was undeserved. So the question of who killed Jesus is an important one to ask. Someone has to answer for condemning the sinless Son of God to a death reserved for the worst of criminals.

Every Person Bears Responsibility for the Death of Jesus Christ

Who crucified Jesus? Was it the Jews, or perhaps the Romans? The Bible gives us an unmistakable answer to this question. The prophet Isaiah wrote seven hundred years before Christ, "He was wounded for *our* transgressions, he was bruised for *our* iniquities: the chastisement of *our* peace was upon him; and with his stripes *we* are healed. *All we* like sheep have gone astray; *we* have turned *every one* to his own way; and the LORD hath laid on him the iniquity of *us all*" (Isaiah 53:5-6, emphasis added).

We can't miss the point. The answer to the question of who crucified Jesus is that my sin and your sin and the sin of all people in the world nailed our precious Savior to the cross. He was God's perfect, final substitute Lamb, dying for the sins of the world. If we want to know who was responsible for the death of the Lord Jesus Christ, all we have to do is look in the mirror.

Now I need to follow up on this statement, because many people deny they are culpable in any way for Christ's death since they weren't among those calling for His crucifixion. This is why I want us to look at *what* killed Jesus—that is, the attitudes that nailed Jesus to the bloody cross of Calvary.

When we look at Scripture, it becomes obvious that the conspirators who participated in Jesus' crucifixion reflected attitudes that still corrupt the human heart today. I'm not interested in just answering the historical question of whose hands nailed Jesus to the cross. My concern is to acknowledge those sinful attitudes that can cause us to compromise with sin instead of confronting it.

Did the Jews Kill Jesus?

But before we do this, we need to deal with the issue of whether the Jews killed Jesus. This is not merely an academic question, but one that that has plagued the church and our Jewish friends for hundreds of years, leading to the shedding of much blood and two millennia of hostility and mistrust between Jews and Christians. As far back as the early centuries of the church, Jews were thought by some to be worthy of persecution because they were "Christ-killers."

The late founder of a very old and respected mission to Jews, who received Christ after coming to America, said he remembered his father warning him about the followers of "the crucified one," who would come to their Jewish community in Eastern Europe and attack their people. Generations of Jewish boys had to regularly dodge rocks and fists on their way home from school as they were chased by bullies yelling, "Christ-killer!"

Did the Jews kill Jesus? Before you answer that, I want to remind you that His apostles were Jews. Another Jew, the apostle Paul, was the mightiest missionary who ever lived. John the Baptist, the forerunner of the Lord Jesus Christ, was a Jew. The early church was made up of Jews, with no Gentiles at first.

Now indeed one segment of the Jewish community in Jesus' day clamored for His death. But only ignorance or prejudice would blame the Jews as the singular people who are responsible for the crucifixion. We have already seen from God's Word that "the iniquity of us all" sent Jesus to the cross.

Let's point the finger of accusation in the other direction for a minute. I would hate for the entire church of Jesus Christ to be judged by one segment of Christianity. We have more than our share of moral scandals and failures in the church. Little does it behoove us to be pointing fingers at anyone else.

We also need to be clear on this: The anti-Semitism that has stained our world does not originate from the crucifixion of Jesus, but from the wicked hearts of sinful men. Anti-Semitism, like all racism, is a distortion of the truth that needs to be condemned in all of its forms. As we said above, Jews have suffered unmentionable persecution for two thousand years. This is a crime and a cancer that never seems to heal.

But put it down big and bold: The cross does not teach hatred against Jews. The cross teaches love, reconciliation, and mercy. No Christian can ever hate anyone for whom Jesus died. And by the way, we are living in a day when God's chosen people need our blessing. God said to Abraham concerning the Jews, "I will bless them that bless thee, and curse him that curseth thee" (Genesis 12:3). That has never been rescinded!

Did the Romans Crucify Jesus?

Did they? Well, the fact is that Jesus was crucified under Roman authority with Roman officials acting as judge and executioner. Those Jewish authorities who wanted Jesus dead took Him to Pilate on that first Good Friday because they were an occupied people who did not have the legal authority to execute anyone. And the soldiers who carried out Jesus' crucifixion were, in a sense, only pawns obeying orders that came from higher up; so we cannot blame them solely.

What about Pilate, that compromising, pussyfooting politician who tried to wash his lily-white hands and protest his innocence (Matthew 27:24)? Was Pilate alone guilty of the crucifixion of Jesus Christ?

We know the answer. Not the Jews alone. Not the Romans alone. Our sins were the nails that held Jesus to the cross, and our hard hearts were the hammers that drove those nails into His sinless flesh. Mel Gibson made an eloquent statement about who crucified Jesus when he put himself in the film—his hand held the hammer that drove the spikes into Jesus. Gibson was saying by that act, "My sin nailed Jesus Christ to the cross." And we could put our hands around his in the same confession.

SINFUL HUMAN ATTITUDES NAILED JESUS TO THE CROSS

Now that we know the who of Christ's crucifixion, we are ready for the what—the attitudes that made the cross necessary. What hellish inclinations in the human heart caused Jesus to be crucified? The answers are found at the foot of the cross itself, for God arranged that a cross-section of humanity was there when Jesus died. We are going to look at Matthew 27 and call the roll of the sin that lurks in the human heart—and let's not be surprised when we find our names on the list. I see in Matthew's account of the crucifixion at least seven attitudes that nailed Jesus to the cross.

Self-Righteous Religion Crucified Jesus

Religion without true repentance and change of heart is a dangerous thing. For evidence of this, we need look no further than the opening verses of Matthew 27. God's Word says, "When the morning was come, all the chief priests and elders of the people took counsel against Jesus to put him to death: And when they had bound him, they led him away, and delivered him to Pontius Pilate the governor" (vv. 1-2).

These priests and elders were the religious leaders of Israel. Many of them were Pharisees, who were the most religious of the religious. They kept the Sabbath with such care that they would not even eat an egg that a chicken had laid on Saturday. They would not kill a flea on Saturday lest they be accused of hunting on the Sabbath. If they got a tack in the sole of their shoe, they could not take it out on the Sabbath lest they be accused of working. This was a religious crowd, but they still arrested Jesus and condemned Him to death.

Many people trudge into churches every Sunday in America and go through ritual and formality, sing songs and give offerings. They are religious but lost. There are people with a chest full of pins for years of perfect Sunday school attendance who have never received Jesus and are on their way to hell. They have religion, but they don't have righteousness. They have Christian culture, but they don't have Christ.

If you were to go to an old sawmill and watch them saw a log, you would see them run that log through the saw again and again until it was perfectly square and straight. But if you were to look at the end of that log, you would see that the heart was still crooked.

That describes the Pharisees. They lopped off this practice and that problem until they appeared outwardly to be straight and good. But God looks at the heart (1 Samuel 16:7). Religion has never saved anybody. Most of the church people in our culture need to turn from religion to Jesus Christ. All self-righteous religion ever did was crucify Jesus. If religion could have saved anyone, Jesus never would have had to die. But self-righteous religion was not alone in nailing Jesus to the cross.

Cold-Eyed Hypocrisy Crucified Jesus

The self-righteous leaders had help in taking Jesus. We read in Matthew 27:3-5: "Then Judas, which had betrayed him, when he saw that he was condemned, repented himself, and brought again the thirty pieces of silver to the chief priests and elders, saying, I have sinned in that I have betrayed the innocent blood. And they said, What is that to us? see thou to that. And he cast down the pieces of silver in the temple, and departed, and went and hanged himself."

Why did Judas, one of Jesus' hand-chosen twelve apostles, betray his Lord unto death for thirty pieces of silver? Well, there are no ifs, ands, or buts about it. Judas was a first-class hypocrite. Judas never lost his salvation; he never had it. The Bible says, "Jesus knew from the beginning who they were that believed not, and who should betray him" (John 6:64).

One of the problems with hypocrisy is that it's easy to hide it behind a mask of spirituality. In fact, the Greek word for *hypocrite* referred to an actor in a Greek drama or tragedy who wore a mask so he could play several different parts.

Look at the apostles. They were so deceived by Judas that they elected him treasurer of the group, even though he was a thief (John 12:6)! Even at the Last Supper, when Jesus handed the bread to Judas to identify him as the betrayer, the other disciples still didn't realize that Judas was the one (John 13:26-30).

But the real danger of hypocrisy is what it does to others around the hypocrite. Some people will miss heaven because they have judged Christianity on the basis of what they see in some hypocrite. But what these people don't understand, or refuse to admit, is that there always have been and always will be hypocrites in every area of life.

Don't judge the faith of our Lord Jesus Christ by the actions of a hypocrite, a counterfeit Christian. Why do people counterfeit money? Because the real thing is so valuable. People don't counterfeit chewing gum wrappers. Every counterfeit Christian is a testimony to the worth and the validity of the real.

Don't let some hypocrite like Judas keep you out of heaven. Anytime you hear people tell about a hypocrite they know and say that all Christians are like that, be sure that this is a lie right out of hell. Every now and then somebody comes to me and says, "Pastor, do you know there are hypocrites in the church?"

Yes, I know there are hypocrites in the church. But let me tell you, there were eleven other apostles who did not stop serving Jesus because of Judas. Someone may say, "Well, I don't want to go to church because it's filled with hypocrites." But, friend, if you refuse Jesus you'll be in hell forever with every one of them. Don't let a hypocrite keep you from Christ.

I said that cold-eyed hypocrisy crucified Jesus because it's almost impossible to be a well-meaning, sincere, right-hearted hypocrite. Now it's true that Judas was eaten up with guilt and remorse after he betrayed Jesus. He took his blood money back to the temple and threw it down, hoping to rid himself of the guilt, just as Pilate attempted to do by washing his hands.

Matthew said Judas hanged himself, although according to Acts 1:18 his corpse fell down and burst open. Judas attempted to escape the hell within him, but he stepped into the hell before him. He found a precipice somewhere, tied a rope around his neck, and jumped off. His body hung there for days until it was bloated and the skin began to crack. Doubtless, it was covered with flies. At last it became so putrid that when he was finally cut down, Judas' body burst open when he fell upon the rocks beneath.

You say, "Adrian, that's not very pretty." I didn't mean it to be pretty. Sin is ugly and putrid. Sin slays and then condemns the sinner to hell. Judas may have appeared to be repentant, but the Bible says, "Godly sorrow worketh repentance to salvation not to be repented of: but the sorrow of the world worketh death" (2 Corinthians 7:10). Judas' hypocrisy drove him to the brow of a hill, not to the feet of Jesus.

Cowardly Compromise Crucified Jesus

I said earlier that the Roman governor of Judea, Pontius Pilate, was a fence-straddling politician. He was a supreme compromiser whose refusal to take a stand made his name forever infamous in the pages of Scripture and history.

Jesus was an uncomfortable reality to Pilate. He had Jesus on his hands and a crowd demanding action. Pilate had to do something with Jesus; so he began by questioning Him. "Jesus stood before the governor: and the governor asked him, saying, Art thou the King of the Jews? And Jesus said unto him, Thou sayest. And when he was accused of the chief priests and elders, he answered nothing. Then said Pilate unto him, Hearest thou not how many things they witness against thee? And he answered him to never a word; insomuch that the governor marvelled greatly" (Matthew 27:11-14).

Pilate just couldn't get Jesus off his hands. He really wanted to release Him because he knew Jesus' accusers had brought Him out of envy (v. 18). So he offered to release either Jesus or Barabbas for the Passover feast, according to his custom, hoping the people would choose Jesus and get him off the hook. But the religious leaders instructed the crowd to ask for Barabbas. Pilate washed his hands in an effort to declare his innocence, but then made the cowardly choice to release Barabbas and have Jesus flogged (vv. 15-26).

Pilate sinned because he was a coward. He had questioned Jesus himself and found Him innocent, and he was shrewd enough to know that Jesus was the victim of jealous enemies. Besides this, God sent Pilate's wife a disturbing dream, and she warned her husband not to do anything to Jesus (v. 19).

But Pilate refused to listen to the voices of reason or of revelation. His conscience also told him that Jesus had done nothing wrong. But when it came time to decide, Pilate listened to the wrong voices. John says that when Pilate wanted to release Jesus, the crowd cried out, "If thou let this man go, thou art not Caesar's friend" (John 19:12).

This gave Pilate a start because he was a servant of the Roman government, and disloyalty meant death. In the end Pilate listened to those who said, "Pilate, if you don't play along with us and crucify this man, we are going to accuse you of treason against Caesar, because this man says he is a king. You know that whoever claims to be a king is the enemy of Caesar. And we'll be sure the news gets back to Rome that you lined up with somebody who is trying to dethrone Caesar."

Pilate knew he was doing wrong when he handed Jesus over to the soldiers, but he was afraid of stirring things up and maybe losing his post. He wanted peace and comfort at all costs. Whatever buttered his bread determined his conduct.

Pilate was like so many people today who explain their compromises by saying, "Well, a man's got to live." No, he doesn't. He has to die and then face God. Pilate tried to make no decision at all, but indecision is often the worst decision. Jesus said, "He that is not with me is against me" (Luke 11:23).

We cannot refuse to make a decision about Jesus because of what it might cost us without peril to our souls. Many people think that by compromising and staying on safe ground, they can have the best of both choices. But the things that Pilate tried to keep, he lost. The robe that adorned his back soon adorned somebody else's back. The gavel that he held in his politician's hand was soon held by another hand. The position that he coveted, he lost. History tells us he died of suicide.

Because he was a coward, Pilate would not take a stand for Jesus. When I invite people to give their hearts to Jesus, I know that the devil will intimidate them with fear. Revelation 21:8 speaks of those who are going to hell, and number one on the list—even before those who refuse to believe—is "the fearful." "The fear of man bringeth a snare" (Proverbs 29:25).

Thoughtless Conformity Crucified Jesus

Well, the crowd around the cross is getting larger as we encounter more people and see the attitudes that crucified Jesus. I find a fourth such attitude in Matthew 27:20, where we read, "The chief priests and elders persuaded the multitude that they should ask [for] Barabbas, and destroy Jesus." The crowd did this in response to Pilate's offer to release a prisoner of their choice in celebration of the Passover.

Now it is doubtful if the people there that day fully realized all that was happening and how important their choice really was. If you had been there and asked one of the people in that crowd why he chose Barabbas and called for Jesus to be crucified, I'm sure he would have said, "Well, I don't really know. But that's what our leaders told us to do, and I believe they know best. Besides, everyone else is screaming for Jesus' death; it's better for me if I just go along with the crowd."

In other words, these people were thoughtless conformers. Just going along with the crowd is a way of life for a lot of people. But I want to tell you, the crowd is almost always wrong! Most of the crowd is going to hell, because "Wide is the gate, and broad is the way, that leadeth to destruction, and many there be which go in thereat" (Matthew 7:13).

The people who spoke up for Barabbas and against Jesus were just taking the broad and easy road. You say, "Well, they didn't know better." That may be true, but ignorance is not innocence. They *could* have and *should* have known better. Others knew better.

The biggest cult in America is the cult of conformity. You can listen to the crowd and form your opinions from the polls of the day, or you can say, "I will follow Jesus, come what may."

Hard-hearted Cruelty Crucified Jesus

Pilate's failure to win Jesus' release led to His being handed over to the soldiers to be tortured and crucified. I want to quote this heart-breaking scene in full as cruel and hard-hearted Roman executioners got their hands on Jesus:

> *Then the soldiers of the governor took Jesus into the common hall, and gathered unto him the whole band of soldiers. And they stripped him, and put on him a scarlet robe. And when they had platted a crown of thorns, they put it upon his head, and a reed in his right hand: and they bowed the knee before him, and mocked him, saying, Hail,*

king of the Jews! And they spit upon him, and took the reed, and smote him on the head. And after that they had mocked him, they took the robe off from him, and put his own raiment on him, and led him away to crucify him. (Matthew 27:27-31)

The reed the soldiers used to beat Jesus was not some thin stalk. It refers to a bamboo club. It is hard to believe the cruelty, but Scripture states it plainly. The soldiers who brutalized and beat Jesus were hard-hearted men in whom the milk of human kindness had curdled.

We live in a world like that today. Some people are absolutely coldhearted, especially when it comes to Jesus and His crucifixion. One nationally known television commentator was reported to have answered when asked if he was going to see *The Passion of the Christ,* "I wouldn't waste nine dollars for a few laughs." May God have mercy upon a heart so hard that it considers Jesus' dying in agony and blood to be laughable. A person can be hard-hearted without actually killing someone. The soldiers at the cross represent the hard-hearted cruelty that crucified Jesus.

Casual Indifference Crucified Jesus

A large crowd of people followed Jesus to the cross, and not all of them were harboring hatred or murder in their hearts. Many were casual observers who, according to Matthew 27:36, simply sat down and watched Jesus being crucified.

Who are these people today? They're the ones who will watch a film like *The Passion of the Christ* while they eat popcorn, leave the theater saying, "That was a pretty good film," and go home completely unchanged. They may have felt bad or had sentimental thoughts about Jesus. They may even have shed a tear or two, but that's as far as it goes. The general crowd at

Jesus' crucifixion didn't openly oppose Him, but neither did they speak up to protest or try to prevent His death.

It takes more than sentimentality or crocodile tears to change a life. Some people come to church every Sunday, listen to the message, and maybe make a few notes. But it never changes their lives. They have no more inclination to obey God than they would to be changed by something they saw the night before on television. Beware of complacency, because it also played a part in crucifying Jesus.

Cynical Skepticism Crucified Jesus

The final group of people at the cross were the skeptics and the cynics who taunted and mocked the Lord Jesus as He hung in agony. Matthew described them:

> They that passed by reviled him, wagging their heads, and saying, Thou that destroyest the temple, and buildest it in three days, save thyself. If thou be the Son of God, come down from the cross. Likewise also the chief priests mocking him, with the scribes and the elders, said, He saved others; himself he cannot save. If he be the King of Israel, let him now come down from the cross, and we will believe him. He trusted in God; let him deliver him now, if he will have him: for he said, I am the Son of God. The thieves also, which were crucified with him, cast the same in his teeth. (27:39-44)

These cynics misquoted Jesus' words about the temple, for He was speaking of the temple of His body. They mocked His deity, saying, "If You are the Son of God . . ." Then they minimized His death by taunting Him to come down from the cross and save Himself.

A cynic is somebody who knows the price of everything and the value of nothing. A person is not a sinner because he is a skeptic. He is a skeptic because he is a sinner. Cynicism comes out of the heart.

Someone says, "Well, I have intellectual problems with the cross." No, you don't. You have rotten sin. "Take heed, brethren, lest there be in any of you an evil heart of unbelief," the Bible warns (Hebrews 3:12).

Someone else says, "Well, I can't believe." No, you *will* not believe. You choose not to believe.

Still another person says, "I know some intellectuals who don't believe the Bible, and some fools who believe it." Well, I know some intellectuals who do believe the Bible and some fools who don't. What other people do has nothing to do with my choice to believe God. The gospel of Jesus Christ is not contrary to reason, but it is *beyond* reason. It would be tragic if a man let his skepticism take him to hell. I often tell Christians that it's OK to doubt, but make sure you are quicker to doubt your doubts than you are to doubt God.

JESUS DIED TO SAVE US

In spite of all of those attitudes and all those people who helped hold the nails and hammers that pinned Jesus to the cross, God allowed His darling Son to die in agony and blood to save sinful people like us. The Bible says in Romans 8:32 that God "spared not his own Son." What really was happening at the cross?

God Judged Sin at the Cross

The cross was judgment at its surest. Think about this. If God did not spare His Son from the judgment of the cross when the sin of the entire world was put upon Jesus, what makes any of us think God will spare us if we reject Jesus and stand before

Him with our sin still upon us? The cross was God's full and final judgment against sin.

God Proved His Love at the Cross

The cross is also love at its greatest. If there were ever a promise that God would have wanted to renege on, or a time when He would say, "I've changed my mind," it would be His promise to send Jesus to the cross to die for our sins. But God kept His promise and did not spare His Son.

God's Grace Was on Display at the Cross

The cross is also grace at its fullest. The rest of Romans 8:32 says that since God "delivered him [Jesus] up for us all, how shall he not with him also freely give us all things?"

If God would give us Jesus, there's nothing else He would withhold. With Jesus, we get everything. Here is amazing love and abounding grace toward those who crucified Jesus, for each and every one of us is guilty of the blood of Jesus. Praise God for the cross.

3

WHAT IS THE GOSPEL?

We're asking and attempting to answer some very crucial questions about the passion—the suffering and death—of our Lord Jesus Christ. In my mind these are the most important questions to ask, because they deal with the eternal destiny of every person who has ever lived. And so we need to ask, what is the gospel? This is an important question because the Bible says that all who believe the gospel will be saved, while all who disbelieve will be condemned.

We need to know what the gospel is not only because it carries eternal weight, but also because the word *gospel* is so often carelessly used, both inside and outside the church. We've all heard someone make a statement and then say, "That's the gospel truth." What the person said may indeed be true, but it has nothing to do with the gospel of Jesus Christ.

A classic example of the misuse of this glorious word occurred some years ago when a popular men's quartet left the gospel music circuit (which often does not have much gospel in it) to break into country music.

When the announcement of the switch was made, a member

of the group's band at that time was asked by a reporter how the change from gospel to country music would affect their "message" (my quotation marks).

This young man answered immediately. "Oh, we're still preaching the gospel," he said enthusiastically. "But now our gospel is to keep people entertained."

You may say, "Adrian, that's a terrible perversion of the gospel," and I agree. But even folks who are sincere in wanting to share Christ often confuse the issue of what the gospel is and what it promises. I heard about a pastor who was trying to determine whether a woman who had come to his church was really a believer.

"Oh, yes," she replied, "I gave my heart to Christ, and I'm trusting Him to heal my marriage." This made the pastor curious, so he questioned her a little further. It came out that some well-meaning person had told this woman that if she would only come to Christ, He could heal her marriage that was falling apart. She wanted that more than anything; so she prayed a prayer and got "saved."

Now is it true that God can heal a marriage? Absolutely. And can many believers testify that once they got saved, their lives and families were restored? Of course. But is the gospel offer, "Come to Christ and He will heal your marriage"? No, it is not.

This pastor said he feared what would happen to this woman's faith if her marriage fell apart. And sure enough, she came back to him several months later, furious at God because her husband had left her. Her "faith" was shipwrecked because as far as she was concerned, God had not kept His half of the bargain.

THE SIMPLE TRUTH OF THE GOSPEL

Dear reader, stories like these make it imperative that we be crystal-clear about the nature and message of the gospel. And the wonderful thing is that the gospel is plain and simple. Paul tells us exactly what it is in 1 Corinthians 15:1-4. We will deal with these verses, but let me summarize them up front by saying that the gospel, plain and simple, is the death, burial, and resurrection of Jesus Christ.

The Gospel Draws a Clear Line Through the Human Heart

The reason that the film *The Passion of the Christ* stirred so many emotions both before and after it was released is that the film's central focus was the death of Jesus Christ for our sins. This simple, and simply wonderful, fact brought the critics and gospel-haters out from under the rocks. Many of the Hollywood elite railed against the message of the film and threatened to blacklist Mel Gibson.

One head of a movie studio, who would not allow his name to be used, said of Gibson, "I won't hire him. I won't support anything he is a part of." The *Dallas Morning News* trotted out liberal theologians who denied that Christ's death was a sacrificial atonement for sin. One New Testament "scholar" said, "It makes God sound bloodthirsty."

You and I know that these attacks and slurs were really not against Mel Gibson or his film, but against the gospel itself. Opposition to the gospel did not begin with the making of this film, and it will not cease now that the film has had its run and is sitting on shelves in stores and movie rental centers.

The apostles were brought before the authorities and commanded "not to speak at all nor teach in the name of Jesus" (Acts 4:18). Paul said, "We preach Christ crucified, unto the Jews a stumblingblock, and unto the Greeks foolishness" (1 Corinthians 1:23). Thank God, the Bible goes on to say, "But unto them which are called, both Jews and Greeks,

Christ the power of God, and the wisdom of God" (v. 24). This is the gospel.

The Gospel Is Very Good News

The word *gospel* literally means "good news." It is the good news of the death, burial, and resurrection of Jesus Christ. The best news this world ever heard came from a graveyard outside Jerusalem: "He is risen; he is not here" (Mark 16:6).

Now good news is not good unless there's the possibility of bad news. Suppose a neighbor called you one day at work and said, "I have good news for you. Your house is not on fire." Instead of responding, "How wonderful," most of us would think the caller was a little strange for thinking that we needed that news at that particular moment.

But your reaction to a call like that would be totally different if you were a couple of hundred miles down the road, or in the air, on the way to your dream vacation and suddenly remembered you'd left the gas on at home. You'd probably be on the edge of your seat until the neighbor you called to check the house and turn off the gas called back to say there was no fire and everything was fine. That would be good news.

A young minister of music at a church in Dallas was recently in the delivery room with his wife as she began labor with their second child. His cell phone rang, and he stepped out into the hall to answer it. It was a friend calling to say their house had been struck by lightning and was on fire.

This dear brother was so startled he repeated out loud, "Our house is on fire!" His wife heard it and became very distraught even as she tried to deliver her baby.

Now that fire was very bad news, but there was some very good news too. This couple praised God that their baby girl was delivered safely that day and that because of the birth neither they nor their other little girl were home when the fire struck. They also found out the fire was contained inside the house, so the roof was intact. And the family moved back into a beautifully rebuilt and remodeled home several months later.

My point is that good news is only good if there is the possibility of bad news. And it's only when we hear the extent of the bad news that we can fully appreciate the good news. The bad news of our condition that makes the gospel such good news is found in verse 3 of our primary text, 1 Corinthians 15: "Christ died for our sins."

People don't like the idea of sin. The evolutionist says we have not yet had adequate time to develop properly. Give us enough time and we will stumble upward and be all right. The geneticist says the problem is in the genes and chromosomes. Maybe one day we can make some designer babies and do away with the problem of sin. The sociologist says the problem is in the environment. Change the environment, and people will change. The educator says the problem is ignorance. If we can just provide everyone with a quality education, people will be enlightened and will quit behaving badly.

All of these approaches deal with what we lack. But our problem is not what we lack—it's what we have. Our hearts are infested and corrupted by sin. And sin brings debt, defilement, and domination.

What *debt* does sin bring? Heaven has sued us for damages. We have misused God's intention for us, and we are in debt to a holy God. Sin also brings *defilement*, for the problem is not only what we have done, but what we are. We are sinners by nature as well as by choice. Therefore sin brings *domination*. It rules over us in our natural state so completely that we couldn't choose the right even if we wanted to.

This is the bad news of sin—and it is bad indeed. Sin is so bad that the gospel and nothing else has the answer for it. That's why Paul said in 1 Corinthians 15:3, "I delivered unto you *first of all* that which I also received" (emphasis added).

The apostle was not saying that the gospel is first chronologically but first in importance. It is the main thing because no matter what else you do, if you don't get the gospel right you have missed it all. Preachers in training are told that the main thing in preaching is to keep the main thing the main thing, and the main thing is the gospel. There are three things I want to show you about the gospel that we must understand if we are to think rightly about this subject that is of primary importance to the church.

THE SCRIPTURAL CONTENT OF THE GOSPEL

Paul declared that the gospel is "according to the Scriptures." The Scriptures of Paul's day were the Old Testament Scriptures. One more time we are reminded that the gospel is not an afterthought or an emergency solution to a problem that arose. The Old Testament had prophesied the gospel, and Paul knew it.

We have seen that the gospel is good news about the death, burial, and resurrection of Jesus Christ. Let's dig deeper into this as we seek to answer the question, what is the gospel?

One of the main contentions of those who do not believe the gospel is that Jesus' death was not necessary to pay for sin. He died merely as an example to show us how to die, these critics say. Well, I'm more interested in what the Bible says.

Jesus' Death Deals with the Debt of Sin

According to God's Word, sin demands the death penalty. "The wages of sin is death" (Romans 6:23). "The soul that sinneth, it shall die" (Ezekiel 18:20). Someone has to die to pay for sin. Either we are going to trust Jesus' death to pay for our sins, or we will pay for them ourselves by suffering the eternal death of hell.

Jesus' death was necessary to deal with the debt that our sin has incurred against God. We read it again in verse 3 of our text: "Christ died for our sins." His death was a blood sacrifice and atonement for sin. Nothing can wash away our sins but the blood of Jesus.

Jesus' Burial Deals with the Defilement of Sin

Most Christians believe and understand that Jesus' death on the cross was in payment for our sins. But many people wonder why Paul included Jesus' burial as an essential part of the gospel. Well, one reason is so we would know for certain that He was dead.

Now lest you think this is simply stating the obvious, I need to remind you that some people have tried to argue that Jesus never actually died on the cross. He only fainted, and the coolness of the tomb revived Him, they say.

This theory says that Jesus then shook off the effects of all those beatings, the loss of blood from six hours of being nailed to a cross, and suffering a spear wound near His heart, then unwrapped His own grave clothes, moved a stone that weighed almost two tons, overcame a detachment of as many as sixteen heavily armed Roman guards, and escaped! Ridiculous, isn't it?

The critics say that Jesus faked His death, and His disciples went along with the ruse even though they knew that their preaching about His resurrection was a lie. The only problem is that they were willing to die for the gospel, and few people are willing to die for a lie when they know it's a lie.

There was no fainting at the crucifixion and subsequent reviving in the tomb. Jesus was buried to prove that He died on Calvary. But there is another reason His burial is part of the gospel. Jesus was buried to show us that God has dealt with the defilement of sin.

You see, just as Jesus' sinless human body was buried in the grave, so our old sinful man was buried with Him. This is what Paul pictured in Romans 6:3-4 when he said that we are "buried with Christ by baptism." This doesn't mean baptism saves us. Baptism is a symbol or picture of our burial with Christ. When a dead body is buried, the defilement of that corpse is buried with it.

As far as the defilement of sin is concerned, it is buried. The great hymn "Rock of Ages" says, "Be of sin the double cure, save from wrath, and make me pure." The debt and defilement of sin are dealt with in the death and burial of Jesus.

Jesus' Resurrection Deals with the Domination of Sin

Here is the third aspect of the gospel's scriptural content, and it is just as wonderful. Paul said that Jesus "was buried, and . . . rose again the third day according to the scriptures" (1 Corinthians 15:4). Jesus' resurrection deals with sin's domination.

If all Jesus did was pay my sin-debt and put my sin in the grave, I am still left with me—I am not changed. So Jesus rose again to save me from the domination as well as the debt and defilement of sin. Romans 6:4 says, "As Christ was raised up from the dead by the glory of the Father, even so we also should walk in newness of life." It is Christ's resurrection power that gives you and me the power to overcome the enslaving power of sin.

This is important because no other religious leader can offer the power of a resurrected life. The resurrection of Jesus Christ was God's stamp of approval upon Christ as the true and only Savior of the world. Someone has called it God's "receipt" proving that our sins are taken away.

When you buy merchandise at a store, you are handed a

receipt that contains the date, time, and other details of that transaction. The receipt shows that the merchandise was paid for in full and that you legitimately own it. Most stores will not take back merchandise without proof of purchase. Why? Because anybody can find or steal something and bring it to a store to say they are returning it and want a refund. But the receipt separates the true owner from the false.

There is an important verse in Romans 4 that we tend to read over quickly. The Bible says that Jesus "was delivered for our offences, and was raised again for our justification" (v. 25). That little preposition "for" can also be translated "on account of," and many Bible teachers believe that is Paul's meaning here. We were justified because Jesus was raised. That is, His resurrection is the proof that God accepted His payment for our sins. The empty grave is God's eternal receipt that we have eternal life! If you want to stop for a while and praise God, go ahead. I'll wait for you!

Many false messiahs and religious leaders have come and gone. Anyone can claim to be God. But the difference between every false god and Jesus is that He is alive. Buddha lived and died. Confucius lived and died. Mohammad lived and died. Jesus lived and died *and rose again.* We serve a risen Savior.

Now let's do a little grammar study. When Paul said Jesus died and was buried (1 Corinthians 15:3-4), those Greek verbs are in the aorist tense, which means something that is done once for all and finished with. Jesus will never die or be buried again.

But when the Bible says, "He rose again" (v. 4), that is literally "He was raised." This is the Greek present tense, signifying an action whose effect continues. This means that Jesus *was* raised from the dead, still *is* raised, and *always will be* raised.

That's very important because no one can run from Jesus. People say they have a date with destiny. No, they have a date with Deity. Every person will meet the risen Christ, either in salvation or in judgment. Jesus died; that's finished. He was buried; that's finished. But He *is* alive forevermore.

THE SAVING INTENT OF THE GOSPEL

The intent or purpose of the gospel is the second aspect I want us to consider. Paul began 1 Corinthians 15 by writing, "Moreover, brethren, I declare unto you the gospel which I preached unto you, which also ye have received, and wherein ye stand; by which also ye are saved, if ye keep in memory what I preached unto you, unless ye have believed in vain."

Believe the Gospel and Be Saved

The intent God has for the gospel is as straightforward and unambiguous as the gospel itself. First of all, the intent of the gospel is that you would believe it and be saved. You can do nothing with the gospel if you don't believe it. The Bible teaches, "Believe on the Lord Jesus Christ, and thou shalt be saved" (Acts 16:31). Romans 1:16 says, "For I am not ashamed of the gospel of Christ: for it is the power of God unto salvation to every one that believeth."

There are many dead ends that people try rather than putting their faith in Jesus. The Bible says, "There is a way that seemeth right unto a man, but the end thereof are the ways of death" (Proverbs 16:25).

One of these dead ends is sincerity. People say, "It doesn't matter what you believe, as long as you're sincere." I beg to differ. You can be sincere but sincerely wrong. The famous comic strip character Charlie Brown once stood on the pitcher's mound with his woeful little team of kids and a dog named Snoopy around him and cried, "How can we lose when we're so sincere?" Because sincerity isn't enough.

Sulfuric acid H_2SO_4 and water (H_2O) are both clear and odorless. But if you drink sulfuric acid rather than water, even if you're sincere in thinking that the acid is water, you'll be sincerely dead. Somebody wrote a humorous poem that says, "Poor Willie, he's gone from us. His face we'll see no more. For what he thought was H_2O was H_2SO_4." Sincerity is not enough. Some of the most sincere people on earth are members of false cults that are leading others away from the truth.

A close cousin of sincerity is sentiment. Judging by their actions, some people must think they can cry their way into heaven. They weep whenever something religious touches their emotions or when they hear a sad story from a speaker. Or they may weep with regret over their sins, but unless that emotion is accompanied by repentance, it is merely "the sorrow of the world [that] worketh death" (2 Corinthians 7:10).

Other people try to save themselves by service. They are working themselves to exhaustion in an effort to please God and earn their way into heaven. But all that service apart from salvation will get you is a plot in the local cemetery and separation from Christ for eternity. Service cannot save.

And then there are people who think that sacraments can save them. But no priest's words spoken over a wafer or cup of wine can imbue those elements with saving power.

There is no salvation apart from Christ. And only the gospel tells us the plain and simple truth about how to be saved. The gospel is not so high and mysterious that few will get up to it. It is so simple that few will get down to it.

Believe the Gospel and Be Strengthened

The gospel is not only strong enough to get you to heaven, but is able to keep you strong in Christ until you get there.

Once again a look at Greek grammar will help us. The verb in the phrase "by which also ye are saved" (1 Corinthians 15:2) is in the present tense, which signifies continuous action. We could translate it literally, "By which ye are being saved." In other words, your salvation is saving you today as much as it did the day you received Christ.

You see, salvation comes in three tenses. I *have been saved* from the penalty and the pollution of sin. I *am being saved* day by day from the power of sin because the gospel is "the power of God." And someday I *will be saved* from the very presence of sin when Jesus returns to take me home to heaven with Him.

Jesus Christ is saving me day by day. This is why I can be strong in Him. Let's stop right here for a moment. If Jesus were not my security now and forever, then the devil or anyone else could come along and steal my salvation from me. It has been many years since as a teenager I asked the Lord Jesus Christ to come into my heart and life. And after all these years, I know beyond a shadow of a doubt that I would never have made it had it not been for the gospel of Jesus Christ that has saved me and strengthens me. Salvation is a crisis when we trust Christ, but that crisis is followed by a process as He pours His life into us day by day.

You don't have to worry about whether you can live the Christian life. You can't! And neither can I. Nobody has ever lived the Christian life except Jesus Christ, and He will live it in and through you.

Believe the Gospel and Be Secured

Did you notice the word "stand" in 1 Corinthians 15:1? This is your security in Christ, and mine. It's great to know that we can be saved. It's greater to know that we can know we're saved. But greatest of all is to know that we can be saved and know we're saved and know that we can never, ever lose our salvation. We stand secure in the gospel.

We sing, "I stand amazed in the presence of Jesus the

Nazarene." We should also sing, "I stand *assured* in the presence of Jesus the Nazarene." The Bible calls the gospel "the everlasting gospel" (Revelation 14:6). Our salvation is for eternity, and no power on earth or under it can change that.

Friend, if our salvation depends on our staying faithful to Christ every moment, we are in bad shape. I wouldn't trust the best fifteen minutes I ever lived to get me to heaven. I am secured by the gospel of the Lord Jesus Christ. I stand assured and secured by the gospel of our Lord and Savior, Jesus Christ. He has me in His hand.

What good is a salvation that is not for eternity? Imagine someone gives you, say, a small key that would be easy to mislay or lose track of and adds this warning: "This is the most precious gift you could ever be given. Hang on to it the best you can for as long as you live. It's your only way into heaven, and if you lose it, you'll be lost forever."

I don't know about you, but I don't want a gift like that. Our security is in Jesus Christ, not in what we do. He is holding us, not vice versa.

Someone asks, "But what if you slip through His fingers?"

That's not going to happen, because I'm one of His fingers! I'm in His body. For me to perish, a part of Christ would have to perish. It is impossible for a twice-born child of God ever again to be a lost soul.

THE SUBLIME EXTENT OF THE GOSPEL

The saving intent of the gospel is as glorious as its simple truth and scriptural content. I also want to touch on the subject of what we could call the gospel's sublime extent. We are going to deal with this issue in depth in the following chapter, so I just want to make some preliminary points.

Notice in our text that Paul said he preached the gospel to

the people of Corinth. In fact, everywhere he went he preached the gospel to anyone who would listen. He did not limit his message to a certain class of people. There are good reasons why Jesus commanded us to take the gospel to the ends of the earth, even to "every creature" (Mark 16:15).

The Gospel Extends to Every Person

This is the crux of the matter that the next chapter will discuss. But let me declare here that the gospel is for all people. God wants "all [to] come to repentance" (2 Peter 3:9). He wants to save all. The Bible's last invitation is, "Whosoever will, let him take the water of life freely" (Revelation 22:17). There is nobody God cannot save and will not save if he or she repents of sin.

The Gospel Extends to Every Place

You don't have to be saved in the front of a church. You can be saved on a street corner or in a submarine.

Some people want to add to the gospel of Jesus Christ. For instance, they may say that in order to be saved, you have to believe on Jesus and then be baptized.

Now, I believe in baptism so much that I'm called a Baptist. But baptism can't save. It is a visible testimony to the invisible transaction in the heart. If you make baptism necessary to salvation, you take the "whosoever" out of the Bible.

I was on an airplane once with a man who belonged to a denomination that believes baptism is necessary to be saved. He was a very kind man, and we had a wonderful conversation about the Bible. At one point I asked him, "Do you ever share your faith?" He said he did.

So I replied, "Let's imagine that I'm sitting next to you on an airplane, just like we're doing now. You tell me you're a Christian and discover that I am not. We're talking when all of a sudden the pilot comes on the plane's intercom and announces, 'Ladies and gentlemen, we have lost all power. The flight crew will prepare you for a crash landing. We have only about five minutes left in the air.'"

With this hypothetical scene set, I went on to ask this man, "Now suppose I panic and tell you I'm a lost sinner who doesn't know Christ, and I don't want to die and go to hell. I beg you to tell me how to be saved. What would you say?"

This man thought for a minute and then started slowly, "Well . . . uh . . . there are certain things you have to do."

I said, "Hurry! We only have two and a half minutes left. How can I be saved?"

After hemming and hawing for another minute, my seatmate on that airplane had to admit he wasn't sure what he would say to a person in that situation. Is that not sad? You see, if baptism is necessary to salvation, a man on a plane that is nose-diving to the ground can't be saved. The gospel is not, "Whoever believes on the Lord Jesus Christ and is fortunate enough to be near water and have a preacher there to baptize him will be saved." The gospel will save anybody in any place.

The Gospel Extends to Every Problem

Finally, the gospel can deal with any problem we could ever have. People say, "I'd like to be saved, but you don't know what I've done. You don't know all the problems I have."

When someone tells me that, I can answer, "My friend, what you have done is not the issue. The only thing that matters is what Jesus has done for you on the cross." Don't let problems keep you from the cross.

What is the gospel? It is the saving power of God to anyone and everyone who believes—with no catches, no conditions, and no exceptions!

4

How Wide Is God's Mercy?

We have thought about the depth of God's love, but let us now consider the width of that mighty love. This is a very serious consideration. The question is this: Is God's love wide enough to encompass the entire human race?

I do not think I would get much disagreement that loving one person and not the other, or giving special advantages to one and not to all, is simply wrong. Let me ask you a question then. Does it make it better if the one showing the partiality is our great God?

Let me make a statement that may surprise some of you. Some people very seriously and honestly believe the Bible teaches that God does not love everybody and that Jesus died only for a select group and not for the whole world. These people believe that the circle of God's love is not wide but is narrowly drawn around His own choice.

This theology is taught in some seminaries and in many churches. It says that God has a chosen few whom He loves, known as the elect, while the rest of the world lies outside the scope of His redeeming love in Jesus Christ. Those whom God loves, and for whom Jesus died, are predestined for heaven. But those who are not loved by God—that is, the non-elect—have no chance of ever going to heaven. The gospel is not good news for them. No matter what happens or what they do, the non-elect cannot be saved. This position is often called limited atonement because it teaches that Christ's death was limited to the few who are God's elect.

I want us to consider a powerful statement by the apostle Paul in 2 Corinthians 5:11-21 that clearly refutes the view of a limited atonement and shows the wideness of God's love:

Knowing therefore the terror of the Lord, we persuade men; but we are made manifest unto God; and I trust also are made manifest in your consciences. For we commend not ourselves again unto you, but give you occasion to glory on our behalf, that ye may have somewhat to answer them which glory in appearance, and not in heart. For whether we be beside ourselves, it is to God: or whether we be sober, it is for your cause. For the love of Christ constraineth us; because we thus judge, that if one died for all, then were all dead: And that he died for all, that they which live should not henceforth live unto themselves, but unto him which died for them, and rose again. Wherefore henceforth know we no man after the flesh: yea, though we have known Christ after the flesh, yet now henceforth know we him no more. Therefore if any man be in Christ, he is a new creature: old things are passed away; behold, all things are become new. And all things are of God, who hath reconciled us to himself by Jesus Christ, and hath given to us the ministry of reconciliation; To wit, that God was in Christ, reconciling the world unto himself, not imputing their trespasses unto them; and hath committed unto us the word of reconciliation. Now then we are ambassadors for Christ, as though God did beseech you by us: we pray you in Christ's stead, be ye reconciled to God. For he hath made him to be sin for us, who knew no sin; that we might be made the righteousness of God in him.

Paul was accused of being unbalanced because of his passion to share Jesus Christ with every person. He was judged to be "beside himself." His zeal was seen as fanaticism. Yet it was the passion of the cross that motivated and compelled Paul and made him the world's mightiest missionary. He knew that Jesus died for all and that all potentially could be saved.

I saw in a Houston newspaper a strange photograph. A woman had her ear pressed on a man's chest. The man had received a heart transplant, and that woman's son's heart was beating in that man's chest. If you were to put your ear on Paul's chest, you would hear the heartbeat of a loving God for every lost soul.

Let me share some vital reasons from this passage that show the wideness of God's love and the power of His passion to redeem every lost soul.

GOD WANTS EVERYONE TO BE SAVED

I want to say that I reject the kind of theology that limits the atonement with all of the unction, function, and emotion of my soul. God wants everybody to be saved. I can say with the apostle Paul, "The love of Christ constraineth us; because we thus judge, that if one died for all, then were all dead: and that he died for all" (2 Corinthians 5:14-15).

Man's Ability to Choose God Does Not Diminish His Sovereign Power

You may have heard theological terms such as God's sovereignty, foreknowledge, predestination, and election used in connection with this issue of how far the grace of God reaches into the world of lost people. Each one of these is a biblical doctrine that I believe.

The Bible teaches that God is sovereign; that is, nothing

could ever happen that is outside of His firm and absolute control. The Bible also teaches that God is all-knowing. Nothing escapes His knowledge; so therefore His foreknowledge is complete. There are no surprises to God, including the choices made by those who accept and reject His offer of salvation in Christ.

From God's viewpoint the past, present, and future are seen at the same time. He knows the choices that people will make. Now people can argue about whether God *saw* beforehand what you and I as free moral agents would do or whether He *fixed that choice* for us before we were ever born. But the fact is that whichever position you take, it does not cancel out the sovereign power of God.

God's Sovereign Power Does Not Diminish Man's Responsibility

There is a balancing truth that we are responsible for our choices. In this passage Paul is pleading for the right choice to be made that would bring reconciliation between God and men.

Perhaps the best example of this in Scripture is found in Peter's sermon on the Day of Pentecost. He told his hearers concerning Jesus, "Him, being delivered by the determinate counsel and foreknowledge of God, ye have taken, and by wicked hands have crucified and slain" (Acts 2:23). Did God know ahead of time that Jesus would be crucified? Of course. Jesus is "the Lamb slain from the foundation of the world" (Revelation 13:8). Did that relieve His crucifiers of their responsibility? Not in the least. Peter called them to repent (Acts 2:38).

The problem with those who take the position that God loves and Christ died only for the elect is that they take part of the truth and make it all the truth. And when you take part of the truth and try to make it all the truth, it becomes an untruth.

Another question of the wideness of God's love involves predestination, which we must believe because the Bible teaches it. But the Bible does not use this term in the way many people think of it. This doctrine is often misunderstood and misinterpreted to mean that God has already decided everything that is going to happen down to the smallest detail of life, and so therefore human beings have no choices to make because our lives are totally predetermined. All we can do is live out the plans already made for us.

The word *predestine* in some form is only used four times in the New Testament, all by the apostle Paul (Romans 8:29-30; Ephesians 1:5, 11). Read these verses and you will see that God's predestination has to do with His determination that those who come to Christ are predestined to be adopted into His family and conformed to the image of Christ.

What about the doctrine of election? Again, I believe in God's elect. But as I read the Bible, I do not see where it teaches that God pre-selects some to salvation and consigns the rest of humanity to eternal damnation without ever making them a sincere offer of forgiveness.

Now in all fairness, some of the people who believe that God loves only His elect and sent Jesus to die for them alone are missionaries and soul-winners, and I thank God for that. But taken to its extreme, this belief is deadening to evangelism and crippling to soul-winning. I want to show you from the Word of God why I believe He wants every precious soul on the face of this earth to be saved.

CHRIST'S LOVE FOR PEOPLE IS UNBOUNDED

If Jesus died for all, as the Bible says, is it such a stretch to also believe that He loves all (2 Corinthians 5:14)? In other words, can you or I walk up to any person anywhere on earth and say without stutter, stammer, doubt, or qualification, "God loves you"? Yes, we can.

God Loves the World of Sinful People

The message of John 3:16 is one of the first truths that children learn in Sunday school. "For God so loved the world, that he gave his only begotten Son, that whosoever believeth in him should not perish, but have everlasting life."

I remember being in Los Angeles one time back in the days of hippies. I was walking down the street when I saw a hippie coming toward me. He had the beads, the clothes, the whole thing. So I thought I would try something. As we passed, I said to him, "Do you have a moment?"

He said, "Yeah, man."

I said, "May I tell you something? God loves you and has a wonderful plan for your life."

He said, "Groovy, man!" and walked off.

Well, it *is* "groovy" that God loves everyone! Those people who believe contrariwise would say that Jesus was talking only about the "world" of the elect in John 3:16 and would interpret His words to mean, "God so loved His elect."

Only God's Grace and Mercy Caused Him to Love Us

That's a clear statement of the limited atonement position, but it isn't what the Bible says. Jesus said that God loved *the world.* We're not to add or to subtract from the Word of God. You don't have to do any fancy theological footwork to believe that God loves everyone and Jesus died for everyone. All you have to do is take the Bible for what it says.

One argument that some make for their position is that since there is nothing in any of us that would merit God's love, the fact that He elected any at all is an act of grace. I also believe there is nothing in us to make God love us. But there *is* something in God that causes Him to love us—His infinite grace and mercy.

Is Jesus talking only about the world of the elect in John 3:16? The context argues otherwise, particularly verses 19-20: "And this is the condemnation, that light is come into the world, and men loved darkness rather than light, because their deeds were evil. For every one that doeth evil hateth the light, neither cometh to the light, lest his deeds should be reproved." Jesus was talking about the world of sin and darkness. This is the world God loves and out of which He is seeking souls who have been mired in the filth of sin but who are of infinite value to Him.

I once read about an elegant woman walking the streets of Paris, dressed in all of her finery. She had a very beautiful diamond ring on her finger, but when she pulled off her glove, the ring came off and fell in the gutter with all of its slime and filthy water.

The woman tried to retrieve her ring using the crook of her umbrella, but she couldn't get it. So finally this elegant woman took off her other glove, pushed her skirts aside, got down on her knees, and put her delicate hand down into that slimy, filthy water. Why? Because a diamond was down there!

We need to treat every soul the way that elegant woman treated her diamond. I don't care who people are or where they are—they are precious to the Lord Jesus Christ. Some people may be lying in the gutter, but they are worth rescuing because God loves them with His unbounded love.

CHRIST'S ATONEMENT FOR PEOPLE IS UNLIMITED

It follows as inescapably as night follows day that if God loves everyone, then He sent Jesus to die for everyone. His atonement is not limited to a few, but is *un*limited to all.

We read above Paul's statement about the wideness of God's love in 2 Corinthians 5:14-15: "The love of Christ constraineth us; because we thus judge, that if one died for all, then were all dead: and [we thus judge] that he died for all."

It Is Important That Jesus Died for All

Let's follow the apostle's reasoning in this verse. He was convinced that because Jesus died for all men, therefore all men were dead and needed the gospel. If you turn this verse around and say that the "one," who is Jesus, did *not* die for all, then it's possible to argue that all people are *not* dead in sin and need salvation. But the Bible refutes that idea from beginning to end. "We have before proved both Jews and Gentiles, that they are all under sin," Paul concluded (Romans 3:9).

If we read further on in 2 Corinthians 5, we come to this statement: "All things are of God, who hath reconciled us to himself by Jesus Christ, and hath given to us the ministry of reconciliation; to wit, that God was in Christ, reconciling the world unto himself" (vv. 18-19). Jesus died for the elect, beyond the shadow of any doubt. He died for all who are saved, because there is no salvation in any other name but the name of Jesus (Acts 4:12). But Jesus also died for *all*.

I have a pastor friend who believes that Jesus only died for the elect and that the only way sinners can be saved is for God to put faith in them first of all—the argument being that since not all people are saved, that means God did not elect to grant the gift of faith to those who are lost.

I said to this dear friend one day, "Would you give me a verse from the Bible—just one verse, not two, three, or four—that says Jesus died only for the elect?"

He pulled a quarter out of his pocket and replied, "If I asked you to get water out of this quarter, could you do it?"

I said, "No."

"The only way to get water out of this quarter is for someone to put water into it in the first place, right?"

I agreed with him.

"So," he concluded, "if a man is totally depraved, the only way faith could come out of that man is for God to put the faith in him first of all, isn't that true?"

I said, "Absolutely. And the Bible says in Romans 12:3, 'God hath dealt to every man the measure of faith.' It also says in John 1:9 that Christ is 'the true Light, which lighteth every man that cometh into the world.' Now put your quarter back in your pocket and give me my verse." I'm still waiting.

The Bible Says That Jesus Died for All

I am convinced in my soul that the Bible affirms again and again that God's love is wide enough to embrace anyone who will come to Him. Consider these additional Scriptures that speak to the universality of Christ's atonement. John the Baptist said as Jesus passed by one day, "Behold the Lamb of God, which taketh away the sin of the world" (John 1:29).

Now I know that part of the argument in the issue of the extent of Jesus' atonement is what the Bible means by the word *world*. But if language means anything, then *world* used without any qualifiers must be understood as encompassing the entire world of people.

If God didn't want us to understand that Jesus' sacrifice on the cross was for everyone, why didn't John the Baptist say what he meant and declare, "Behold the Lamb of God, which taketh away the sin of those in whom God will place faith because they are His elect"? I don't find any qualifiers or limitations on the Bible's teaching that Jesus died for the world.

Jesus said in John 12:46-48, "I am come a light into the

world, that whosoever believeth on me should not abide in darkness. And if any man hear my words, and believe not, I judge him not: for I came not to judge the world, but to save the world. He that rejecteth me, and receiveth not my words, hath one that judgeth him: the word that I have spoken, the same shall judge him in the last day."

Now this is very interesting. Jesus not only asserted that He came to save the world, but notice what He said about the basis of judgment for those who refuse and reject Him. Those who are lost are lost because they refuse to believe His word, which is the gospel. In other words, unbelievers are condemned because although they heard and were offered the message of salvation, they refused to believe it. They are not condemned because God chose not to activate faith in their hearts.

A passage that poses real problems for those who believe in limited atonement is 1 John 2:2, where the apostle says, "And he [Jesus] is the propitiation for our sins: and not for ours only, but also for the sins of the whole world."

Propitiation is a big word that means the passion of the Christ is a satisfactory payment for our sins. God saw His Son's sacrifice, and His righteous judgment against sin has been satisfied. God's justice is met by the death of Jesus.

Now if Jesus is the propitiation for the sins of the whole world, does that mean everyone is automatically saved? Of course not. I don't know any reputable Bible teacher who believes that. John was saying that Christ's death is sufficient to pay for the sins of the whole world.

This is one point on which both sides of this issue should agree. There is no sinner anywhere at any time whose sin is beyond the power of Christ's blood to redeem. Some say that while Christ's death is sufficient to take away the sin of all, it is only efficient for the elect. That is, it only takes away the sin of those to whom God has previously determined to grant the gift of faith.

Now again, I agree that Jesus' blood saves all those who come to Him in faith. But think what the limited atonement view does to the proclamation of the gospel. If this is true, then as a pastor I have to tell people that although the sure cure for their sin is generally available, I can't tell them for sure that it is actually available *to them*.

Imagine telling a person who is dying of a dreaded disease, "I have good news and not so good news. The good news is that a complete cure for your illness has been found, and there's more than enough of the serum to go around. But the not-so-good news is that you may not be one of the sufferers chosen to receive it and live."

Is that the good news of the gospel? Not as I read the Bible! Instead, I turn to 2 Peter 2:1 and read these words: "But there were false prophets also among the people, even as there shall be false teachers among you, who privily shall bring in damnable heresies, *even denying the Lord that bought them*, and bring upon themselves swift destruction" (emphasis added).

Consider what Peter was saying. We may think of false teachers who deliberately try to lead people from the truth as the worst of sinners. Surely if God wanted to withhold the possibility of salvation from anyone, it would be these mouthpieces of the devil.

But Christ also paid the price for their sins on the cross. The word "bought" in this verse is the Greek term *agorazo*, which means "to buy out of the slave market, to redeem from slavery." Even those false prophets who were teaching "damnable heresies" would find forgiveness if they turned from their sin, for they too had been bought with the precious blood of Christ.

I want to give you two other verses that help seal the case. Paul urged us to pray for "all men," including those in authority (1 Timothy 2:1-2). Then he gave us the reason in verses 3-6: "For this is good and acceptable in the sight of God our Savior;

who will have all men to be saved, and to come unto the knowledge of the truth. For there is one God, and one mediator between God and men, the man Christ Jesus; who gave himself a ransom for all, to be testified in due time." The death of Jesus Christ makes salvation possible for all. Faith in Christ brings it to the heart and achieves it for those who believe.

The writer of Hebrews said, "We see Jesus, who was made a little lower than the angels for the suffering of death, crowned with glory and honour; that he by the grace of God should taste death for every man" (2:9).

Can black print on white paper be clearer? I do not believe these Scriptures teach a limited atonement. Now let me give you another reason why I believe God's love is open wide to all who have sinned.

CHRIST'S INVITATION TO PEOPLE IS UNCONDITIONAL

If God loves all people without exception, and if Jesus died for all without distinction, then we would expect the Bible to invite all to salvation without condition. And that is what we see in 2 Corinthians 5: "All things are of God, who hath reconciled us to himself by Jesus Christ, and hath given to us the ministry of reconciliation; to wit, that God was in Christ, reconciling the world unto himself, not imputing their trespasses unto them; and hath committed unto us the ministry of reconciliation" (vv. 18-19).

God's unbounded love for sinners and Christ's unlimited atonement for sin leads to an unconditional invitation. God has reconciled the world to Himself because we as sinners were at war against God. We are the ones who broke the relationship with God and were at enmity with Him. The Bible is very careful to say that God is the one doing the reconciling, because He is the only one who could do it. He is the offended party, not us.

We can offer an unconditional invitation to the lost with the sure knowledge that God is long on patience. "The Lord is not slack concerning his promise, as some men count slackness; but is long-suffering to us-ward, not willing that any should perish, but that all should come to repentance" (2 Peter 3:9).

God does not want the people of this world to die and go to hell. He wants all people to be saved. If you change the meaning of that, then language loses its ability to communicate with any real accuracy or relevance.

Dear reader, as believers we had better get settled in our minds what we have to offer to a sick and dying world.

We need have no fear of embarrassment when we invite sinners to come and drink freely from the Water of Life because it flows for all. Jesus issued this wonderful invitation: "Come unto me, all ye that labour and are heavy laden, and I will give you rest" (Matthew 11:28).

THE COMMISSION OF CHRIST TO HIS CHURCH IS UNDIMINISHED

We read in 2 Corinthians 5:18 that God has committed the "ministry of reconciliation" to His followers. Paul was even stronger in stating our commission in verse 20: "Now then we are ambassadors for Christ, as though God did beseech you by us: we pray you in Christ's stead, be ye reconciled to God."

Our Commission Is as Wide as the World

Now if God was in Christ reconciling the world to Himself and has given us the message that peace can be made with Him through the blood of Christ, does it not follow that the announcement of this message should reach as far the offense— that is, to the world? I believe this is the only logical conclusion we can draw from these two premises.

The fact that God sends us out as His ambassadors to freely

proclaim salvation to all in no way diminishes God's fore-knowledge or His sovereignty. God still knows the end from the beginning, and He rules over His creation. But God does not force His love on anyone.

There are some who talk about "irresistible grace," the idea that you cannot say no to God. But the Bible tells of many people who resisted God's love. People have the dubious privilege of saying no to God without damaging His eternal attributes one bit.

The commission we have received as Christ's ambassadors is not to decide what Jesus really meant when He said, "Go ye into all the world, and preach the gospel to every creature" (Mark 16:15). Our privilege and responsibility as ambassadors of the King of kings is to go into all the world with the wonderful news that in Christ those who are under a sentence of death can have their death penalty canceled and live. Shame on us if we do not share this message with every person alive.

Our Commission Involves an Urgent Message

Suppose a man is scheduled to be executed for his crime. But you petition the governor, "Please don't allow this man to be executed. There are mitigating circumstances. He should not be put to death."

Now suppose the governor's office investigates the case and agrees. The governor writes a pardon for the condemned man and hands it to you to deliver. You put that pardon in your pocket and leave, but on the way you get a call to finish an important business deal. You forget about that piece of life-giving good news in your pocket as you get involved in the day's affairs.

Pretty soon you've forgotten about the pardon altogether and go off on vacation. But when you get back, you read in the newspaper that the man you were so concerned about was executed. In horror you rush into your closet, tear frantically through the pockets of your coat, and find the pardon still there. You never told the man he was free, and he died.

The Bible says that if we fail to obey God by warning sinners of their sin and the need to turn to God, we are going to be held culpable. God issued this sobering message to Ezekiel:

> *O son of man, I have set thee a watchman unto the house of Israel; therefore thou shalt hear the word at my mouth, and warn them from me. When I say unto the wicked, O wicked man, thou shalt surely die; if thou dost not speak to warn the wicked from his way, that wicked man shall die in his iniquity; but his blood will I require at thine hand. Nevertheless, if thou warn the wicked of his way to turn from it; if he do not turn from his way, he shall die in his iniquity; but thou hast delivered thy soul. (Ezekiel 33:7-9)*

If you believe there is a kind of predestination and election that says people are going to be saved or lost no matter what, this warning makes no sense. As a matter of fact, God would be capricious to hold us responsible for the death of a sinner who was never a candidate for the saving blood of Christ.

As Christ's ambassador, I cannot make anyone accept Him, and praise God that is not my responsibility. I must realize that the people to whom I speak have the privilege to say no, but they also have the blessed opportunity to say yes to Jesus.

C. S. Lewis said the world is divided into two categories: those who, like Satan, say to God, "Not Thy will, but mine be done," and those, who like Jesus, say to the Father, "Not my will, but Thine be done."

All people are in one of these two categories. I thank the Lord that we can freely and joyfully say to all, "Whosoever will may come." This is truly good news.

PART II

THE CENTRALITY OF
THE CROSS
IN CHRIST'S PASSION

5

A PROPHECY OF
HIS PASSION

Now that we have dealt with some of the most crucial questions relating to the passion of the Lord Jesus Christ, it is time to turn our focus toward the cross more fully and to the central role that Jesus' death plays in His passion.

I have mentioned that one strong impetus for my thoughts and studies that resulted in this book was the release of Mel Gibson's incredible film *The Passion of the Christ*. I believe that even someone who had never read the Bible or heard about Jesus could come away from that film with the clear message that whatever else this Jesus was about, His crucifixion on the cross was at the very center and heart of His story.

The cross also stands at the center point of biblical revelation and mankind's redemption. Everything that God revealed prior to the cross pointed forward to Jesus' atoning sacrifice as the Lamb of God who would take away the sin of the world. We are going to study an amazing example of that in this chapter. And everything that God revealed after the cross points back to that literally earthshaking event when Jesus died as the final sacrifice for sin.

As an instrument of torture and death, the cross was invented by the Romans, who ruled Israel in Jesus' day. This helps explain why the cross does not appear in the Old Testament. The Jews executed by stoning, not by hanging someone on a cross made of wood. The saints of ancient days only knew that their Messiah and Redeemer would come and give His life as a ransom for their sins. They did not know exactly the manner of His death, although several Old Testament prophetic passages reveal the brutal nature of Jesus' suffering.

One of these passages is Isaiah 53:1-12, which describes how Jesus was beaten and tortured. These verses are often read and preached on at Easter, and they are amazing in their vividness. But the "Old Testament Calvary" I want us to study in this chapter is a prophetic look at Jesus' crucifixion and its redeeming purpose that was written some nine hundred years before the nails were driven into our Lord's hands. I'm referring to Psalm 22, which is given over almost in its entirety to describing in astounding detail the suffering that Jesus endured on the cross.

The superscription of Psalm 22 attributes it to King David, but it sounds as if it were written by someone standing at the foot of the cross. We have to wonder if David, speaking as a prophet, fully understood what he was writing when the Holy Spirit inspired him to pen, "They pierced my hands and my feet" (v. 16). David had never seen a crucifixion, but by the Spirit of God he was foretelling the means by which Jesus was fixed in such cruel fashion to that cross. Psalm 22 is prophecy, and Jesus Christ fulfilled it down to the smallest detail in His death.

How central is the death of Christ to our faith? So central that it was presented in type, shadow, and prophecy—from the promise of Genesis 3:15 that God would crush Satan's head to the end of the Old Testament. So central that even the method of Jesus' sacrifice was revealed in detail to God's people many centuries before it was fulfilled, so there would be no mistaking that this One who was hanging on a cross on the outskirts of Jerusalem was the promised Savior. Jesus is the central person of the Bible, and the cross stands at the center of Jesus' life and ministry.

The ancient Egyptians who built the great pyramids boasted of themselves, "We build like giants, but we finish like jewelers." That is, they created massive works, but in their work they carefully attended to the smallest detail, like a jeweler carefully cutting a precious stone.

Thus it is with Jesus. The Bible presents God's great work of creation and redemption in its massive, magnificent grandeur. But God is also interested in the smallest detail of His work, especially when it comes to His darling Son. The Bible has but one hero, and His name is Jesus. For our purposes in studying Psalm 22, I have divided it into three distinct parts.

THE PROPHECY OF THE CROSS

The first of these three divisions is what I'm going to call the prophecy of the cross. Through the psalmist David, the cross is prophesied in all of its human horror and ugliness, and yet all of its redeeming glory.

This Is Prophecy in Stunning Detail

We don't have to look long to find examples of prophecy in Psalm 22. It begins with the very words that Jesus Christ would say from the cross: "My God, my God, why hast thou forsaken me?" (v. 1; see Matthew 27:46). Someone may say that Jesus was simply looking backward, quoting from the Psalms that He had learned, to enhance His claim to be the Messiah. But the truth is that David was looking forward, quoting Jesus!

The prophecy continues in Psalm 22:2, where we read, "O my God, I cry in the daytime, but thou hearest not; and in the

night season, and am not silent." Jesus was crucified at nine
o'clock in the morning and died at three in the afternoon.
During the last three hours of His agony, the land was engulfed
in a supernatural darkness. So Jesus cried out to God from the
cross both in the day and in the night, just as prophesied in
Psalm 22.

The Bible says of Jesus' crucifixion, "Now from the sixth
hour there was darkness over all the land unto the ninth hour"
(Matthew 27:45), which is from noon until 3:00 P.M. in the
Jewish reckoning. The heavens were darkened at noonday.
When the Son of God hung on the cross, even the sun in all its
brightness had to hide its face amid the darkness of men's hearts
as Jesus died at cruel hands and bore the filth and stench of all
the world's sins upon Himself. David was precise in his
prophecy.

Now here's something else that's amazing. The critics may
say that Jesus deliberately quoted from the Scripture to make
His death seem Messianic. That's bogus anyway. But what
about the words of His enemies? Could Jesus force them to say
what He wanted them to say to fulfill Scripture? Of course not.

But what do we find in Psalm 22:7-8? David prophesied that
those who ridiculed the Lord Jesus when He was on the cross
would "laugh [Him] to scorn: they shoot out the lip, they shake
the head, saying, He trusted on the LORD that he would deliver
him: let him deliver him, seeing he delighted in him."

Then at Calvary those who stood around the cross watching
"wagg[ed] their heads" as they taunted Jesus, saying, "Thou
that destroyest the temple, and buildest it in three days, save thy-
self. . . . He saved others; himself he cannot save. If he be the
King of Israel, let him now come down from the cross, and we
will believe him. He trusted in God; let him deliver him now, if
he will have him" (Matthew 27:39-43). Jesus' enemies testified
unwittingly to the centrality of the cross.

This Is Prophecy in Agonizing Detail

Psalm 22 continues in verse 14a: "I am poured out like water." When Jesus was on the cross, the Roman soldiers came to break the legs of those hanging there in order to hasten death. They broke the legs of the two thieves being crucified with Jesus, but according to John 19:33, the soldiers did not break Jesus' legs because He was already dead. Instead, John writes as an eyewitness, "One of the soldiers with a spear pierced his side, and forthwith came there out blood and water" (v. 34). The fluid around Jesus' heart was poured out like water.

Physicians say that when fluid builds up around the pericardium, the heart cavity, it is a sign that the victim has been under great, great duress. Jesus literally died of a broken heart. As I studied this, I wondered if the things that break the heart of Jesus break my heart.

But there was more suffering that Jesus endured. "All my bones are out of joint" (Psalm 22:14b). After a person was nailed to a cross, the Romans dropped the cross roughly into a hole. Josephus, the Jewish historian, says that when the cross was dropped, the jolt would wrench the victim's bones out of joint, greatly increasing the pain.

Jesus Christ was also filled with a blistering thirst on the cross, as prophesied in verse 15 of this Psalm: "My strength is dried up like a potsherd; and my tongue cleaveth to my jaws." A potsherd is a broken piece of a vessel—nothing but dried, hardened clay. Jesus was filled with thirst on the cross, and John said of that moment, "Jesus knowing that all things were now accomplished, that the scripture might be fulfilled, saith, I thirst" (John 19:28). The One who made all the oceans and rivers and fountains of water was parched with thirst as He died for you and me.

Notice also how Psalm 22:16 describes those who would

perpetrate the crucifixion. "Dogs have compassed me: the assembly of the wicked have enclosed me."

Who crucified the Lord Jesus? God the Father crucified Him so we could be forgiven of our sins. "Thou hast brought me into the dust of death" (v. 15b) is a reference to God. But the Gentiles also crucified Jesus. The Jews referred to the Gentiles as "dogs," a reference to Pilate and the other Romans who condemned the innocent Son of God to death on the cross.

And what about "the assembly of the wicked"? Here the psalmist was looking ahead to the Jewish council, headed by the cowardly high priest Caiaphas, that found Jesus guilty and demanded His death. They're all there in this prophecy that we are calling an "Old Testament Calvary."

The psalmist even foretold the awful humiliation that Jesus endured as He hung between heaven and earth. "I may tell all my bones: they look and stare upon me" (v. 17). Jesus was stripped of His clothing and hung naked on the cross. He who was perfect purity and undefiled modesty was exposed to the taunts and stares of those around the cross. The Bible says, "And sitting down they watched him there" (Matthew 27:36).

I want to look at one more amazingly precise prophecy in Psalm 22 as we seek to understand the centrality of the cross. According to verse 18, "They part my garments among them, and cast lots upon my vesture."

People wore four minor pieces and one major piece of clothing at that time. The major piece was a woven undergarment, a seamless robe. John 19:23-24 says the soldiers divided Jesus' clothes four ways, with one part for each soldier. But they did not want to tear His seamless robe; so they cast lots, or rolled the dice, to see who would get it. Matthew refers to this very prophecy of Psalm 22:18 being fulfilled at Jesus' crucifixion (27:35).

Why did God lead David to write with such precise detail and incredible accuracy about Jesus' passion? Because the cross was at the very heart of the Father's plan to redeem lost humanity.

THE AGONY OF THE CROSS

I also want us to see the price that Jesus Christ paid for our redemption so that we might be saved, filled with the Holy Spirit, and have a hope that is steadfast and sure. I want us to understand why we ought to praise and serve Christ because of the suffering that He suffered. No one ever suffered like the Lord Jesus Christ. Others were crucified, but nobody ever suffered like Jesus. This is because Jesus not only suffered at the hands of cruel and wicked men—He also suffered at the hands of Satan, and even at the hands of a holy God—His own heavenly Father, with whom He had lived in eternal, unbroken fellowship.

Jesus Suffered at the Hands of a Holy God

The most important aspect of Jesus' suffering is the rejection He had to suffer at the hands of a God who is so holy He cannot look on sin. Jesus cried out in great agony, "My God, my God, why hast thou forsaken me?" The psalmist said, "Thou hast brought me into the dust of death" (Psalm 22:15).

It is a profound mystery why God the Father had to forsake God the Son. I don't understand it, but I believe that God turned His back on His darling Son whom He loved. I also believe that the reason Jesus cried out twice is that He was calling to both the Father and the Holy Spirit—for God is a Trinity of three distinct yet coequal Beings.

Why did God have to turn His back on Jesus as He hung on the cross? We mentioned it above, but the answer is in Psalm 22:3: "But thou art holy."

As Jesus hung on the cross, the heaviest weight that bore

down upon Him was not the suffocating weight of His own body as He struggled to push Himself up on nail-pierced feet in order just to breathe. His greatest agony was not the searing pain of His bloody, laid-open back rubbing against the rough-splintered wood or the unimaginable torture of every socket being ripped out of joint. The greatest weight and agony Jesus carried on the cross was the weight of being our sin-bearer.

Many of us can remember as children when our fathers had to punish us for our wrongdoing. Many a loving father would say, "This is going to hurt me more than it hurts you." We could not imagine how that could be until we became parents and had to punish those little ones who were the joy of our hearts.

Multiply that feeling to an infinite degree, and we still cannot even begin to imagine how much it hurt the heart of God to abandon His innocent Son to suffering and death. The Bible says that God made Jesus, who was without sin, "to be sin for us" (2 Corinthians 5:21). Why? "That we might be made the righteousness of God in him."

Underline that word "*righteousness.*" God is pure righteousness, undiluted holiness, while we are total unrighteousness—and therein lies the problem. The prophet Habakkuk declared, "Thou art of purer eyes than to behold evil, and canst not look on iniquity" (Habakkuk 1:13).

Someone had to pay the penalty for our sin, and the Godhead determined in the councils of eternity that Jesus would be that sin-bearer. Part of the penalty for sin that sinners must bear apart from Christ is to be forsaken of God forever in a devil's hell. God had to forsake His Son there on the cross because at that moment, Jesus was bearing all the ugliness of our sin.

Now someone may say, "Yes, I'm sure that was awful. But Jesus only had to bear the Father's rejection for a short time on the cross." Don't ever get the idea that because Jesus was forsaken by God for a brief time as we count time, therefore it could not be as awful as eternal separation from God.

Nothing could be further from the truth. Let me say it again. Jesus, being infinite, suffered in a finite period of time what you and I, being finite, would suffer in an infinite period of time. Make no mistake about it. Jesus suffered all the eternity of hell in those hours on the cross that you and I would suffer for an eternity if we were cast into hell.

Did God really have to abandon His pure Son to such suffering just to save unworthy sinners like us? Yes, He did, and praise God for the deep, deep love of Jesus! He who had been in the bosom of the Father from eternity past was forsaken of God for our sake. And because Jesus went to the cross, we can say with David, "Yea, though I walk through the valley of the shadow of death, I will fear no evil: for thou art with me; thy rod and thy staff they comfort me" (Psalm 23:4).

But Jesus walked that lonesome valley of death all by Himself, "for the wages of sin is death" (Romans 6:23). Paul said that God "spared not his own Son" (Romans 8:32). Who delivered Jesus to the cross? God delivered Him. Who refused to spare Jesus? God refused to spare Him. Who forsook Jesus? God forsook Him. On the cross, Jesus become the object of His Father's loathing and wrath.

Jesus Died at the Hateful Hands of Men

But Jesus also died at the hateful hands of men. "But I am a worm, and no man; a reproach of men, and despised of the people" (Psalm 22:6). Peter told his audience in his great Pentecost sermon, "Ye have taken [Jesus], and by wicked hands have crucified and slain [Him]" (Acts 2:23).

Consider the humility of Jesus, who willingly submitted Himself to those who trampled Him into the dirt as one would step on a lowly worm. And by the way, His attitude is to be our attitude. "Let this mind be in you, which was also in Christ Jesus: who, being in the form of God, thought it not robbery to be equal with God: but made himself of no reputation, and took upon him the form of a servant . . . and became obedient unto death, even the death of the cross" (Philippians 2:5-8).

The "worm" spoken of in Psalm 22:6 was a grub-like worm that, when crushed, emitted a crimson dye. Amazingly, the word translated as "worm" here is translated as "crimson" in the familiar text of Isaiah 1:18: "Come now, and let us reason together, saith the LORD: though your sins be as scarlet, they shall be as white as snow; though they be red like crimson, the shall be as wool." Thank God that He shed His crimson blood for our crimson sin, so that we might be washed whiter than snow. The crimson blood of the Lord Jesus flowed from His crushed body on the cross as He suffered at the hateful hands of men.

I heard of a father who received a phone call at his desk one day. It was the police. "Sir, we hate to tell you this, but there's been an accident. A young man has been hit by an automobile. We don't have all of the details, but we believe he's your son."

The stunned father asked where the accident was, and when given the address he realized it was near his office. "I'll be right there," he told the officer.

This poor father ran out of his office and drove to the accident site. "Where is the boy who was hit?" he asked an emergency worker. Not knowing to whom he was speaking, the worker said, "You mean the boy who was killed?"

"What!" the father replied in anguish. "Where did it happen?" The worker showed him the place on the street where the boy had been struck. And right there on the street was a fresh pool of blood that this father now knew was his son's. And when he saw the cars on that busy street driving one after another right through that precious blood, the dead boy's father couldn't take it anymore. He tore off his coat and jumped into the street in front of his son's blood, waving his coat and crying in agony, "Stop! Stop! You can't drive through my son's blood like that! I won't let you dishonor the blood of my son!"

Jesus allowed Himself to be stepped on like a worm, and wicked men trampled His blood under their feet. But the Bible warns us not to trample under our feet the precious blood of Jesus Christ (Hebrews 10:29). I don't know of a greater sin than to treat the blood of Christ lightly.

Jesus Suffered at the Hellish Hands of Satan

Once again, as we turn back to Psalm 22, we find another insight into the agony of Jesus' suffering: "Be thou not far from me, O LORD: O my strength, haste thee to help me. Deliver my soul from the sword; my darling from the power of the dog. Save me from the lion's mouth" (vv. 19-21).

We know that the dogs were evil men, but who is the lion? It is Satan himself, that old roaring lion who "walketh about, seeking whom he may devour" (1 Peter 5:8). All the artillery of hell was let loose upon the Lord Jesus when He was on the cross. All the powers of the pit were concentrated upon Him.

Jesus said to those who came out to arrest Him in the Garden of Gethsemane, "This is your hour, and the power of darkness" (Luke 22:53). He was referring to the power of Satan, who put it into Judas' heart to betray Jesus and manipulated the hateful hands of those who took Him, just as a master puppeteer controls the strings of his puppets. Hell had a holiday when Jesus was nailed to the cross. The demons taunted and tormented the Savior. Jesus was abandoned by God, abused by men, and attacked by Satan.

This was the agony of the cross. The sins of the world were

distilled into the bitter cup of agony that Jesus drank to the dregs. The wonder is not that He prayed, "O my Father, if it be possible, let this cup pass from me" (Matthew 26:39). The wonder is that He concluded, "Nevertheless not as I will, but as thou wilt." No one ever suffered like Jesus—no one.

THE VICTORY OF THE CROSS

We have seen the Savior's suffering and rejection in prophecy and in history. And perhaps by this point you may be feeling the pain I felt as the horror and agony of Jesus' suffering unfolded in *The Passion of the Christ*. But if ever there was a story that was not over until it was over, to borrow a popular phrase, it is the story of Jesus. Psalm 22 also tells of the victory of the cross!

Beginning in verse 22 of this great Psalm, the tone changes. To this point the Psalm is going down, down, down as the awful reality of the cross is portrayed. But then the Psalm turns upward suddenly because there is a resurrection. "I will declare thy name unto my brethren: in the midst of the congregation will I praise thee. Ye that fear the LORD, praise him; all ye the seed of Jacob, glorify him; and fear him, all the seed of Israel" (vv. 22-23).

Jesus Is the Prophet Who Declares the Father

Jesus Christ is presented in the Bible as prophet, priest, and king. Here we see Him as prophet, declaring God's name to His people who are gathered in the congregation.

I hope you noticed the phrase "my brethren" in verse 22. Did you know that Jesus calls us His brothers? The writer of Hebrews declared, "For both he that sanctifieth and they who are sanctified are all of one: for which cause he is not ashamed to call them brethren, saying, I will declare thy name unto my brethren, in the midst of the church will I sing praise unto thee" (2:11-12).

Verse 12 is a quote from Psalm 22, which tells us that Jesus, the eternal God, is a close relation to us. I am next of kin to the Trinity—and so are you. We're family. Jesus Christ meets with us, His people, when we meet. He sings with us when we sing (that truth should revolutionize our song services!) and receives our praises.

Jesus Is the Priest Who Delivers the Faithful

As our High Priest, Jesus also delivers the faithful. "The meek shall eat and be satisfied: they shall praise the LORD that seek him: your heart shall live for ever" (Psalm 22:26). As priest, Jesus leads the people in declaring God's praises. The priests of Israel offered the showbread (Exodus 25:30), which represents Jesus, the Bread of Life who feeds His people. Jesus is ready to give anyone who asks Him the bread of life that sustains the soul forever.

Jesus Is the King Who Dominates the Future

Here is the ultimate victory of Calvary. When He comes as King to take His rightful throne, Jesus shall reign forever and ever. The psalmist wrote, "All the ends of the world shall remember and turn unto the LORD: all the kindreds of the nations shall worship before thee. For the kingdom is the LORD's: and he is the governor among the nations" (Psalm 22:27-28). Jesus is the Potentate who is going to dominate the future.

People say, "What's the world coming to?" I can tell you what the world is coming to. It's coming to Jesus! Jesus owns this world. It was made by Him and for Him, and the Bible says He's coming back to claim it as His kingdom. On that glorious day, "the kingdoms of this world [will] become the kingdoms of our Lord, and of his Christ; and he shall reign for ever and ever" (Revelation 11:15).

Jesus is prophet, priest, and king. And at the center of this divine drama of redemption, rescue, and rule stands the cross of Christ.

6

GOD'S CRUCIFIED LAMB

S ome years ago the sports media told the story of a boy who had been born into a home where his father was determined to do whatever was necessary to mold him into a football star.

Now, millions of American fathers have harbored dreams of athletic greatness for their sons, and many of them have pushed their boys to excel in some sport. But this dad was different. He was a fitness expert and fanatic, and from the moment of his son's birth, he dictated and oversaw every aspect of the boy's life, from diet to workout regimens. The boy was not allowed to have what most people would consider a normal childhood. His every waking moment was focused on turning him into a football superstar.

By the time the sports media began following the story, the boy had grown into a strapping teenager, 6'4" tall, with a strong passing arm. His father came under criticism for treating his son like a laboratory rat in an experiment, but he shrugged it off.

It looked for a while as if his experiment might pay off. His son became a star quarterback in high school and won a scholarship to the University of Southern California, one of the most prestigious college football programs in the country. By then he was also the object of intense media attention.

But then things started to go wrong. The young man was good, but not a superstar. At one point he got into trouble with drugs. And though he had a chance to play pro football, he didn't make the grade, and his name faded into oblivion.

Most parents would rebel, and rightly so, at the idea of bringing a child into the world with the idea of preparing him to do only one thing. But heaven's Parent, God the Father, sent His Son Jesus Christ into this world to do one thing—to offer Himself as "the Lamb of God" who takes away the sin of the world. I want us to explore the rich biblical theme of Jesus as the sacrificial, substitutionary Lamb slain for your sin and for mine. This study reveals yet another facet of the wonderful truth that the cross stands at the center of God's plan to redeem a fallen race.

The earthly story of God's crucified Lamb begins, of course, with Jesus' birth in Bethlehem. You can read the very familiar story in Luke 2:1-7. Mary had her little Lamb in a stable. For now let's turn our attention to another familiar part of the Christmas story:

> *And there were in the same country shepherds abiding in the field, keeping watch over their flock by night. And, lo, the angel of the Lord came upon them, and the glory of the Lord shone round about them: and they were sore afraid. And the angel said unto them, Fear not: for, behold, I bring you good tidings of great joy, which shall be to all people. For unto you is born this day in the city of David a Saviour, which is Christ the Lord. (Luke 2:8-11)*

It was not incidental or accidental that Jesus was born in Bethlehem, a little village about five miles south of Jerusalem.

Bethlehem was the hometown of David. So Jesus' birth there showed Him to be David's greater Son, Israel's Messiah, whose birth had been foretold centuries before by the prophet Micah: "But thou, Bethlehem Ephratah, though thou be little among the thousands of Judah, yet out of thee shall he come forth unto me that is to be ruler in Israel; whose goings forth have been from of old, from everlasting" (Micah 5:2).

It was also fitting that Mary's Lamb would be born in Bethlehem, because for centuries the Jewish priests had been raising lambs for the Jewish Passover in Bethlehem. The shepherds in those fields outside Bethlehem who learned of Jesus' birth that night were watching over a very special breed of sacrificial lambs. These lambs were being raised and nurtured for just one purpose: to be perfect and without blemish and thus qualify to be offered at the Passover. There in Bethlehem God's perfect Lamb, the Lord Jesus, was born. The destiny of this world is wrapped up in Jesus, the Lamb of God.

Now you may be wondering how we got from Christmas to Passover in talking about Jesus' birth. We'll see how as we discuss what I'm going to call the prophecy of the Lamb. For in reality the story of Jesus as God's crucified Lamb who saves His people from their sins begins not in Bethlehem but almost fifteen hundred years earlier in the land of Egypt.

WE SEE JESUS CHRIST IN THE PROPHECY OF THE LAMB

The book of Exodus tells the story of how the family of Jacob, or Israel, grew into a great nation in Egypt after going there from Canaan to escape a terrible famine (see the last few chapters of Genesis). The Egyptians came to fear the Hebrews so much that they enslaved them. So when the deliverer Moses was sent to Egypt to lead God's people out, he came to a people who were living in slavery under cruel taskmasters.

The Israelites needed to be redeemed from the hand of Pharaoh and brought into their own land. And when the time was right, God put into action His plan to redeem His people and set them free. This plan was wrapped up in the sacrifice of a little lamb—and thus we see *the* Lamb, the Lord Jesus, in prophecy.

In Exodus 12 God gave Moses the instructions needed to prepare the Israelites for redemption:

> *Speak ye unto all the congregation of Israel, saying, In the tenth day of this month they shall take to them every man a lamb, according to the house of their fathers, a lamb for an house. . . . Your lamb shall be without blemish, a male of the first year: ye shall take it out from the sheep, or from the goats: And ye shall keep it up until the fourteenth day of the same month: and the whole assembly of the congregation of Israel shall kill it in the evening. (vv. 3-6)*

Now think about this scene. The Israelites are slaves to the most powerful monarch and kingdom on earth. And how does God announce that He is going to deliver them? He is going to use a lamb, the most gentle, meek, and defenseless of all the creatures on earth. A lamb has no fangs or claws to defend itself with, and it cannot outrun its predators. A lamb is a symbol of gentleness, submission, and weakness. A lamb seems to present itself to the slaughter.

I heard about a man who worked in a slaughterhouse where they butchered cattle. This man thought nothing of his job until one day the slaughterhouse began to process lambs. When a lamb came through the chute, he said it was his responsibility to cut the lamb's throat.

"I had never done that before," he said. "It didn't bother me to watch cattle wrestle and fight, but that little lamb just lay his neck back. I put in the knife, and the blood came out onto my hand. That lamb looked up at me and then licked the blood from my hand. I laid down my knife right there and resigned my job."

By contrast, the symbol of ancient Egypt was a serpent. When I visited the British Museum in London, I was eager to see the section on Egyptology. I saw the crown that the Pharaoh wore, with a serpent coiled upon it. The Pharaoh's scepter also had a serpent coiled on the end of it. From a human standpoint, a defenseless, gentle lamb would have no chance of victory in a battle with a powerful, poisonous, hissing serpent. But this was no ordinary lamb, for this was the Lamb of God in prophecy.

This Was a Special Lamb

The lambs that the Israelites were to choose for this first Passover were to be without any blemish at all. One flaw would disqualify an animal.

Later the priests in Israel very carefully examined the lambs being considered for the Passover. They would look inside the lamb's mouth and examine the eyelids and the ears for any sign of a blemish. Only a perfect lamb could speak of the coming Lamb of God, the Lord Jesus, who was a Lamb "without blemish and without spot" (1 Peter 1:19).

This Was a Slain Lamb

This special Passover lamb was chosen for death. The Israelites in Egypt were to select their lambs on the tenth day of the month and slay them four days later. The father in an Israelite family would lift back the head of that lamb, cut its throat with a swift, merciful cut, and catch the blood in a basin. The Bible says this was to take place "in the evening."

Here's an amazing thing. This was to take place at 3:00 in the afternoon, the very time of day that, so many years later,

Jesus would die on the cross as God's crucified Lamb to pay for the sin of the world. What a prophecy of the Lamb we see in Exodus 12!

This Was a Saving Lamb

God continued His instructions to Israel by saying:

> *And they shall take of the blood and strike it on the two side posts and on the upper doorpost of the houses, wherein they shall eat it. . . . For I will pass through the land of Egypt this night, and will smite all the firstborn in the land of Egypt, both man and beast; and against all the gods of Egypt I will execute judgment: I am the LORD. And the blood shall be to you for a token upon the houses where ye are: and when I see the blood, I will pass over you, and the plague shall not be upon you to destroy you, when I smite the land of Egypt. (Exodus 12:7, 12-13)*

Here is the story of the first Passover. As long as the residents of any Israelite house obeyed God's command and posted the blood of the lamb on their dwelling, and as long as they stayed inside that night under the protection of the blood, they were safe from the hand of God's death angel. God's promise of deliverance was, "When I see the blood, I will pass over you."

Salvation does not come from the life of Christ but from His death. Salvation is not learning lessons from the life of Christ, but receiving life from His death. The blood of Jesus must be applied to your life to take away your sin, for as we learned earlier, the inescapable truth of the Bible is, "Without shedding of blood is no remission [for sin]" (Hebrews 9:22).

This Was a Shared Lamb

A final glimpse at God's crucified Lamb in prophecy shows us that He was a shared lamb. God commanded the Israelites to eat all of the lamb together in a shared meal. Anyone who refused to join in the Passover meal would forfeit the salvation that the lamb brought.

The Passover lamb was roasted (Exodus 12:8), which speaks of Jesus' enduring the fires of God's wrath for us. Jesus' soul experienced agony in hell for us.

Can you imagine what it must have been like that night in Egypt? The Egyptians must have smelled those roasting lambs. Some estimate that as many as a quarter of a million lambs were roasted in Israelite homes that night. Each family, or group of families if they were small, shared the lamb that had shed its blood to deliver them from death. And as they walked out of Egypt, a lamb walked out inside of them.

We are also to walk with the Lamb inside of us. It is receiving Christ into our hearts that saves us from our sins. The Bible says, "Christ in you [is] the hope of glory" (Colossians 1:27). It is Christ in you who gives you the strength to live for Him. We are to feed upon Him day by day. Seeing the Lamb of God in prophecy is an awesome sight indeed!

WE SEE JESUS CHRIST IN THE HISTORY OF THE LAMB

The Lamb who was portrayed in prophecy became a fact of history when Jesus was born of Mary. John the Baptist's followers knew there was something very special about Jesus the day John pointed to Jesus and said, "Behold the Lamb of God, which taketh away the sins of the world" (John 1:29).

And again the next day John saw Jesus and cried out, "Behold the Lamb of God!" (v. 36). Andrew and John, two of the Baptist's disciples, understood instantly that Jesus was God's Passover Lamb who would be slain for the sins of the world, and they began to follow Jesus (v. 37).

Jesus Was a Special Lamb

Andrew and John realized that Jesus was a special Lamb, just like the spotless lambs that were being offered every Passover in Jerusalem. Jesus was without blemish, the virgin-born Son of God.

Someone might say, "Well, I believe a virgin birth is an impossibility." I do too; but I also believe that with God, all things are possible. The little baby wrapped in swaddling clothes lying in a manger in Bethlehem was and is the eternal, uncreated, self-existent God become flesh. "The Word was made flesh," the apostle John testified (John 1:14). The Infinite became an infant.

Jesus Was a Slain Lamb

John the Baptist and his disciples did not yet know that Jesus was headed to the cross, but from the earliest days of the Savior's ministry, the cross cast its huge shadow over His life. The cross was not an afterthought with God, but the heart of His eternal plan of redemption. Jesus is "the Lamb slain from the foundation of the world" (Revelation 13:8).

Why was Jesus born of a virgin? So He could be sinless. And why was it necessary that He be sinless? So He could shed His blood in atonement for sin. God's holiness and justice demanded a blood sacrifice in payment for sin, and the only sacrifice God would accept was a sinless one. This is a requirement that no child of Adam could meet, because "in Adam all die" (1 Corinthians 15:22).

A baby's bloodline is not established by the mother but by the father. None of the baby's blood circulates through the mother's body. The mother may have one blood type and the child another. It was necessary that Jesus be born apart from an earthly father so that His blood would be kept free from the contamination of Adam's sin. While Mary was Jesus' earthly mother, God was His Father, and the blood that flowed through Jesus' veins was in a sense the very blood of God.

Jesus Was a Saving Lamb

The power of Jesus' blood shed on the cross to redeem us is such that when Paul made his farewell speech to the elders of the church in Ephesus, he told them, "Take heed therefore unto yourselves, and to all the flock, over which the Holy Ghost hath made you overseers, to feed the church of God, which he hath purchased with His own blood" (Acts 20:28). Jesus bought us with His blood, and now we belong to Him. Nobody else can make this kind of a claim upon us.

The story is told of an orphan boy who had no place to go. A man in the town who was considered rather eccentric took the boy in, even though the man had no wife to help take care of the lad. One day a fire broke out in the man's home, and the boy was trapped on the second floor. Ignoring the flames and the searing pain in his hands, the man clawed his way up a very hot downspout to reach the boy's window. He lifted the boy out of the burning house and carried him down to safety on his shoulders.

Sometime later the man tried to adopt the boy. But many in the town expressed their doubt that he was the best choice to be the boy's guardian, and the case went to court. Some experts on child development argued that the boy would be better off in a different home. The man sat silently and listened to the arguments made against him.

When the judge asked him to present his case, the man didn't say a word. He simply stood up, walked to the front of the courtroom, and held out his hands, which were badly scarred from the burns he had suffered to rescue the boy. Nothing else needed to be said, and he was awarded custody of the boy he loved and wanted to be his son.

Jesus' hands, scarred with the nails that held Him to the cross, revealed His love for us and are the only argument needed to prove that we belong to Him. He ignored the pain and agony of the cross and went readily to Calvary so that He might make us what we are not but ought to be—sons and daughters of God.

The cross occupies such a central place in the Bible's story of redemption that about a third of the Gospels are given over to the last week of Jesus' life. One New Testament scholar even went so far as to say that the Gospels are basically passion narratives with extended introductions. That's an amazing statement, but it's hard to argue with it when much of the Gospels depict the events surrounding Jesus' passion.

When Jesus entered Jerusalem on Palm Sunday (Luke 19:28-44), He went in through the eastern gate. At the same time those Passover lambs that had been born in Bethlehem were coming in through the sheep gate. And later, when Jesus cleansed the temple and began to teach the people, the religious leaders probed and examined Him critically, challenging His authority to do what He did and say what He said (Luke 20:1-8).

In other words, Jesus was being examined in the days leading up to the Passover and His crucifixion on Friday. And at the same time the lambs from Bethlehem were being critically examined by the priests on the temple mount in preparation for their sacrifice at the Passover. Only those that were deemed to be perfect were chosen—and Jesus also passed the test! His enemies had to confess, "Never man spake like this man" (John 7:46). Even Pilate was forced to conclude, "I find in him no fault at all" (John 18:38; see also 19:4, 6).

On that last week of His life, God's crucified Lamb went from the temple mount to the Passover feast and the Last Supper and then out to dark Gethsemane. And at nine o'clock on Friday morning, He was crucified.

Jesus' cross was raised on Mount Moriah, where centuries

earlier God had ordered Abraham to offer his son Isaac as a sacrifice. In answer to Isaac's question about the lamb for the sacrifice, Abraham told him, "God will provide himself a lamb" (Genesis 22:8). And now that word was coming true in a way that Abraham probably could not have fully comprehended.

As God's Lamb hung on the cross, He cried, "It is finished" (John 19:30), "Paid in full." The final Lamb had been sacrificed to pay for the sins of the world. No more animals needed to die to cover sin. The priests could go home. The shepherds on the hills outside of Bethlehem didn't need to raise any more lambs for the Passover, because "Christ our passover is sacrificed for us" (1 Corinthians 5:7). The cross stands at the center point of history as glorious testimony to the truth, "It is finished." Our sin-debt has been paid!

Jesus Was a Shared Lamb

The Israelites gathered under the protection of a lamb's blood and shared a meal of its flesh on that first Passover night in Egypt. As believers today, we come to the Lord's Table in communion, which means sharing, to partake together of His flesh and blood as represented in the elements we receive.

The Israelites celebrated their freedom at their meal, and we too are to celebrate our freedom in Christ as we come to the Lord's Table. When we share the Lamb, we don't come to mourn a corpse—we come to hail a conqueror. That's why I want to talk next about the Lamb in victory.

WE SEE JESUS CHRIST IN THE VICTORY OF THE LAMB

Prophecy and history are done as they relate to the coming of Jesus Christ to die as God's Lamb on the cross to pay for our sins. The glorious reality today is that Jesus is the Lamb in victory.

Beginning in Revelation 4, the apostle John was caught up into heaven and saw a glimpse of glory. He saw the throne of God, and in His right hand was a book sealed with seven seals (5:1). No one was found worthy to open the book, and John began to weep. But then one of the heavenly elders said to him, "Weep not: behold, the Lion of the tribe of Juda, the Root of David, hath prevailed to open the book, and to loose the seven seals thereof" (v. 5).

And then John saw a magnificent vision of the risen, victorious Jesus: "And I beheld, and, lo, in the midst of the throne and of the four beasts and in the midst of the elders, stood a Lamb as it had been slain, having seven horns and seven eyes, which are the seven Spirits of God sent forth into all the earth. And he came and took the book out of the right hand of him that sat upon the throne" (vv. 6-7).

This seven-sealed book is the title deed to the earth, the heavens, and the netherworld. It speaks of the right to rule. No angel in heaven above was able to open the book, and neither was any politician, religionist, scientist, philosopher, or military genius on earth. Neither could Satan or any demon of hell open the book. Only the Lamb was able.

This Is a Small Lamb

Now here is a curious thing. In the midst of this magnificent scene of Jesus' incomparable power and glory, He is called a Lamb. We have already discussed the fact that a lamb symbolizes meekness and defenselessness. But the Greek word in Revelation 5:6 is not even the ordinary word for lamb. It is a diminutive form, picturing a "little lamb" or "pet lamb."

Here again is the symbol of a lamb set against the forces of evil headed by that powerful, hissing serpent Satan and his powerful ruler, the Antichrist, the Beast. Those same forces were arrayed against each other back in Egypt, and the lamb prevailed. Praise God, the Lamb prevails in heaven too.

This Was a Slain Lamb

John saw this Lamb as a slain lamb. Jesus still has the marks of the nails in His hands, and He will bear those scars forever. When I go to heaven, I'll touch the nail prints in His hand, just as He invited Thomas to do (John 20:27). Jesus will be the slain Lamb throughout the endless ages of glory.

This Was a Standing Lamb

Notice also in John's vision that the Lamb is standing. Jesus bent His back to those who beat Him and carried His own cross to Calvary as far as He could (then Simon was forced to carry it the rest of the way). He then lay down on the wood and spread out His hands so they could be nailed. Then He was laid down in death in the grave. But the grave could not hold Him. He stood up and walked out of that tomb! And He is forevermore making intercession for us (Hebrews 7:25). The picture of Jesus standing in heaven speaks of the resurrection and ongoing ministry of the Lamb.

This Was a Strong Lamb

Jesus was crucified in weakness, but He lives again by the power of God {2 Corinthians 13:4). The Lamb that John saw in Revelation 5:6 had seven horns. Horns in the Bible are emblematic of power. An animal would use its horns to ram and gore and overcome its opponent. Seven is the emblem of perfect power. The Lamb of God has been granted all power.

This Was a Searching Lamb

The description of Jesus in His resurrection glory in heaven just keeps getting better. Notice that He also has seven eyes, which the Bible says are "the seven Spirits of God sent forth into all the earth."

Being full of eyes speaks of the Lamb's great wisdom and intelligence—ever probing and searching, impossible to hide from. As the horns are symbolic of Jesus' omnipotence or all-power, so the seven eyes are symbolic of His omniscience (all knowledge). Jesus is the all-knowing Lamb who knows every thought we think and sees every move we make.

This Was a Sovereign Lamb

Finally, Jesus is also pictured in victory as the sovereign Lamb who alone is worthy to take the book from God the Father's hand, break the seals, and reveal its contents.

If someone were to ask Jesus, "What right do You have to take that book?" He would say, "I have every right. The heavens, the earth, and the underworld are Mine because I created them. Then I paid for them on Calvary, and I rose again to conquer death and hell and take My rightful place as Ruler of all. I have every right to rule because I am the great I Am."

How did the awesome, glorious inhabitants of heaven respond to the Lamb? They fell at His feet in worship and adoration and sang this new song: "Thou art worthy to take the book, and to open the seals thereof: for thou wast slain, and hast redeemed us to God by thy blood out of every kindred, and tongue, and people, and nation; and hast made us unto our God kings and priests: and we shall reign on the earth" (Revelation 5:9-10).

All of heaven is bowed in worship, service, and obedience to the Lamb. So the only question remaining is, how should we respond to Jesus? Let me answer in this way.

A young man who was seeking the will of God for his life went to see his pastor. The pastor told him there was an unusual painting of Jesus on the cross on display in a certain gallery in that city and said, "I want you to go see it."

The young man went to the gallery and found the painting.

But he was somewhat confused because the artwork seemed to be out of proportion. He couldn't make sense of the painting; so he asked a guide at the gallery to help him. "Come closer to the painting, and bend down lower," the guide told him.

The young man followed the guide's advice, but still the portrait of Jesus seemed to be out of proportion. "Come closer still, and get lower," the guide said again. The young man inched a little closer. "Come closer still, and get lower," repeated the guide.

The young man kept coming closer to the painting and getting lower until finally he found himself kneeling at the foot of the cross. And when he did, he looked up and everything was in perfect proportion.

We need to do what this young man did. The best response we can make to God's crucified Lamb is to bow at the foot of the cross and look up with submission and total commitment into the face of Jesus.

7

THE WISDOM OF
THE CROSS

One artist has painted a picture of the young man Jesus in His father Joseph's carpenter shop. There on the floor are the wood shavings and sawdust from the day's work. It's toward the end of the day, and the sun is setting. Jesus is standing at the door with His arms on the doorposts, looking at the setting sun. But behind Him you can see that His profile has formed the shadow of a cross on the floor of the shop. Jesus lived in the shadow of the cross. He was born to die.

Let me ask you a question. Have you ever wondered why God determined in the councils of eternity that Jesus Christ would go the cross to suffer and die for our sins? There is profound mystery here, but the answer we are given in God's Word is that this was the Father's holy and perfect will for His Son. The cross may seem foolish to human wisdom, but it is the expression of God's wisdom.

The apostle Paul addressed the issue of God's wisdom versus human wisdom in a very important passage of Scripture we are going to consider in this chapter. Paul had to deal with this issue because the message he preached everywhere was the message of the cross, and he quickly discovered that neither the Gentiles nor the Jews of his day wanted to hear about a crucified Savior.

The cross appeared as foolish to Gentiles, and it was offensive to Jews. But Paul defended his message, writing to the Corinthians, "Christ sent me not to baptize, but to preach the gospel: not with wisdom of words, lest the cross of Christ should be made of none effect. For the preaching of the cross is to them that perish foolishness; but unto us which are saved it is the power of God. For it is written, I will destroy the wisdom of the wise, and will bring to nothing the understanding of the prudent" (1 Corinthians 1:17-19). Take the cross out of the gospel, and Paul had nothing to say.

I love what the British preacher Charles Haddon Spurgeon, one of the greatest pulpiteers who ever lived, said when someone once complained, "All of your sermons sound alike."

"That may be true," Spurgeon responded, "because I take a text anywhere and make a beeline to the cross."

Paul said the cross is not only the centerpiece and heart of the gospel, but it is also the test of whether a person is a fool. According to the Bible, a man's reaction to the cross determines whether he is foolish or wise. The fool rejects the cross as crude and bloody and unnecessary, while the wise man embraces the cross and the Savior who hung upon it. True wisdom is found in the cross.

THE CROSS IS THE SUPREME DIVIDING LINE OF HISTORY

Now I realize that many people today still consider the preaching of the cross to be foolishness. These people are not all out in the secular world either. As we have said before, the controversy surrounding *The Passion of the Christ* brought both friends and foes of the cross before the cameras and microphones. Many of the film's harshest critics were theologians and clergy who want to move Christendom away from the "bloody religion" of the cross.

Some of these critics said the cross was a scandal and an offense, and I agree with them! Paul said in Galatians 5:11 that if he were to preach the way the Judaizers wanted him to preach, and which he was accused of doing, then he wouldn't be persecuted for "the offence of the cross." That word "offence" in Greek is *skandalon*, which you can see is the basis of the English word *scandal*.

Make no mistake about it—it is offensive, even scandalous, to go to proper people and tell them they are destitute sinners on their way to an eternity in hell if they do not run to the foot of Jesus' bloody cross. Therefore those who don't want the church to offend anyone must avoid the cross. What we are seeing today is an attempt to make the church a little more worldly, and the world a little more churchly, in order to take away the shame of the cross.

I don't know of anything that divides the world more neatly or completely into two camps than the cross of Jesus Christ. The cross starts at a different source, follows a different course, and ends at a different destination than the wisdom of this world. What the world calls wisdom, God calls foolishness; and what God calls wisdom, the world calls foolishness.

One way we can see this contrast is in Paul's phrase in 1 Corinthians 1:18, where he called the cross "the power of God." Now to most people a cross hardly suggests power. On the human level there is probably no greater picture of helplessness and weakness than a beaten figure fastened to a wooden cross, barely able to breathe.

You can be sure that Jesus' enemies thought they finally had Him when they saw Him dying on the cross. They must have felt they had heard the last of Jesus when the Roman seal was placed on His tomb. Jesus was definitely crucified in weakness (2 Corinthians 13:4), but He was raised in power.

The devil certainly thought he had won when Jesus went to the cross and then to the grave. Paul wrote in 1 Corinthians 2:6-8 that if "the princes of this world," those who crucified Jesus, had known that He would rise from the dead in victory, they would not have crucified Him. Satan was the most surprised being in the universe when Jesus arose, for the devil thought he had outwitted God by stirring up deadly opposition to Jesus.

But again the devil's perverted wisdom was shown to be total foolishness. "Hath not God made foolish the wisdom of this world? For after that in the wisdom of God the world by wisdom knew not God, it pleased God by the foolishness of preaching to save them that believe" (1 Corinthians 1:20-21).

Paul was not saying that preaching is foolish. This refers to the content of the message as unbelievers perceive it, not to its delivery. The Greek grammar here means, "what the cross preaches." In other words, the cross itself preaches. I want you to see what the cross says to us and to all the world.

THE CROSS IS GOD'S SUPREME WORD OF REVELATION

If you want to know God, you will know Him supremely in the cross of Christ. Now according to Hebrews 1:1-3, God has spoken to mankind in the past in many ways.

For instance, God has spoken in *nature*. If you walk outside at night and look up at the starry heavens, as I love to do, your heart cannot help but soar in praise to God. David said, "The heavens declare the glory of God; and the firmament showeth his handiwork" (Psalm 19:1). God has put the candelabra of the stars in the sky to show what a mighty God He is.

God has also spoken in *history*. I believe that history is really "His story," the story of God and His work in human affairs.

God has also speaks to us in the inner voice of *conscience*. We are made in God's image with an inner longing to know Him that nothing else can satisfy.

But the greatest way that God has spoken to us, and continues to speak, is through *the cross*. The problem is, not everyone is listening. Paul went on in 1 Corinthians to say, "The Jews require a sign, and the Greeks seek after wisdom" (1:22). In other words, neither the Jews nor the Greeks wanted to hear the message of the cross. What was God's answer? "But we preach Christ crucified, unto the Jews a stumblingblock, and unto the Greeks foolishness" (v. 23).

The Jews Were Looking for a New Moses

The Jews of Jesus' day wanted miracles. Their constant refrain to Jesus was, "Show us a miracle, and we will believe You are the Messiah." They were looking for a mighty, miracle-working liberator like Moses who would free them from their oppressor, the Roman Empire.

The devil knew the Jews were looking for a miraculous sign. That's the reason he tempted Jesus to throw Himself down from the pinnacle of the temple in the sight of all Israel (Matthew 4:5-7). Satan even quoted Psalm 91:11-12 to try and convince Jesus that if He would just jump from that dizzying height, the angels would set Him down safely and everyone would believe in Him. But Jesus knew better, and He wouldn't dance to the devil's tune in any case.

A lot of people believe today that if God would just write the gospel with His finger in the sky, the way the fingers appeared and wrote on the wall at King Belshazzar's party (Daniel 5:5), or perform some other undeniable miracle, the world would be wowed and won to Christ.

But that just isn't true. The best example of that is the rich man of Luke 16:19-31, who begged Abraham to send Lazarus back from the dead to warn his brothers against coming to the place of torment he was in. The rich man was sure his brothers would believe someone who had risen from the dead, but Abraham answered, "If they will not hear Moses and the prophets [the Scriptures], neither will they be persuaded, though one rose from the dead" (v. 31).

If we need further proof, we can go to John 6. Jesus fed five thousand men plus women and children in one of the greatest miracles of His ministry (vv. 1-13). But the very next day some of those same people came to Him and asked, "What sign showest thou then, that we may see, and believe thee? what dost thou work?" (v. 30).

Can you believe that? We would say today, "What's the matter with you people? Are you blind!" These Jews still had the crumbs from the bread they had eaten at Jesus' miraculous meal stuck in the folds of their robes, and here they were demanding a miraculous sign! You get the idea that they weren't honestly seeking the truth about Jesus. In fact, by the end of John 6 all of Jesus' would-be disciples got offended and left Him standing there with just the Twelve (vv. 66-68).

People fill churches and arenas all across America chasing after a miracle. And plenty of preachers go from place to place advertising miracles but never doing them. Jesus did them and didn't advertise them. You need to be very careful when you ask God for a miracle. Why? Because the devil can also perform miracles. Never make your response to God or your belief in Jesus dependent on seeing a miracle. If you do, you sin grievously. Jesus said to a man one day, "Except ye see signs and wonders, ye will not believe" (John 4:48). Jesus was not only rebuking the man but the crowd around him too. The Lord was saying, "You are taking the wrong approach toward Me, and you will not truly believe even if I give you a sign."

Another problem with miracles is that they are like the potato chips in that famous commercial: You can't have just one. A hunger for miracles feeds on itself, and pretty soon people begin expecting them to happen as the normal way of dealing with things. You will probably never hear a preacher who promises a miracle a day say to his audience, "All right, we need to move on now. We have had our quota of miracles." One miracle is never enough.

Jesus must have grown weary of the Jews' constantly pressing Him to do a miracle on demand for them. On one occasion He told a large crowd, "This is an evil generation: they seek a sign; and there shall no sign be given it, but the sign of Jonas the prophet. For as Jonas was a sign unto the Ninevites, so shall also the Son of Man be to this generation" (Luke 11:29-30).

How was Jonah a sign? By spending three days and three nights in the belly of the great fish. Jesus was speaking of His death and resurrection, of course; but that was not the sign the people of Israel wanted to see. Their constant demands for a sign amounted to little more than the demeaning demand, "Come on, Jesus, do a trick for us."

The Greeks Were Looking for a New Socrates

Miracle-mongering was the Jews' problem. They wanted a new Moses to lead them to freedom. But the Greeks, another term for the Gentiles of Jesus' day, were more interested in philosophy than in religious issues. They wanted a new Socrates who would speak great words of wisdom and give them something profound to think about. "The Greeks seek after wisdom" (1 Corinthians 1:22).

The people to whom Paul was referring were the scholars of the day—erudite, sophisticated people who worshiped at the shrine of philosophy and exalted human wisdom. These were people who disdained religious emotionalism as unworthy of people who used their intellect. When Paul spoke to a group of Greeks on Mars Hill, they called him a "babbler" (Acts 17:18), literally a "seed-picker." Studying and discussing philosophy was the major sport among the Greeks.

Now the fact is that these two categories of people are still present in religious circles today. You can turn on the television and find people in flowing robes standing in front of beautiful stained-glass windows, speaking about God in very grave tones and with great sophistication. And yet just a few channels over is a group of people jumping up and down, claiming that all kinds of miracles are occurring in their midst.

Some people are too sophisticated to look for miracles, and others are too superstitious to look to philosophy, but neither one is the answer. But the idea of a suffering and dying Messiah was extremely offensive to the Jews. And the idea of a resurrected Lord was foolishness to the worldly-wise of Paul's day. When he mentioned the resurrection in his great sermon at Athens, most of his hearers started laughing and making fun of him (Acts 17:32).

People Today Need to Be Looking at the Cross

Now don't misunderstand what I am saying. The Bible does not denigrate knowledge or the search for the true meaning of life. Nor does the Bible teach us to be cynical and unbelieving when it comes to God's power to perform miracles. One of the dividing lines between those who believe the Gospels and those who do not is the issue of whether Jesus really performed the miracles that were attributed to Him.

Paul's warning is not to let a desire for miraculous signs or thirst for knowledge blind us to the wisdom of God that is right before our eyes, as it were, in the cross. In contrast to the unbelieving Jews and Greeks, Paul's word to us is, "Unto them which are called, both Jews and Greeks, Christ [is] *the power of God*, and *the wisdom of God*. Because the foolishness of God is wiser than men; and the weakness of God is stronger than men" (1 Corinthians 1:24-25, emphasis added).

Do you see what Paul was saying? He was saying that when we look at the cross, we see the very thing that the Jews and the Greeks were seeking but didn't know where to look. The Jews wanted to see God's power displayed, and the Greeks thirsted for wisdom. And God's Word says in essence, "Look at the cross, and see God's power and wisdom displayed in the seeming foolishness of a Savior hanging in weakness and suffering on the cross."

Do you want to see power at work? Look at the power of the crucified and risen Lord to transform a life. At the beginning of his letter to the Romans, Paul wrote, "I am not ashamed of the gospel of Christ: for it is the power of God unto salvation to every one that believeth; to the Jew first, and also to the Greek" (1:16). Isn't that interesting? Seekers of power and wisdom can both find satisfaction in the gospel.

I know how people are. If we were to bring a crippled child onto the platform at our church in Memphis and heal that child dramatically, radically, and completely, beyond the shadow of any doubt, we would not be able to handle the crowds that would come the next Sunday, to say nothing of the media. And if I issued a call for people who wanted Jesus to change their lives, I have no doubt that the aisles would be filled with seekers.

But I can also assure you that if no miraculous healing was forthcoming the next week, or the week after that, the crowds would soon start to thin out. The television networks would pull their reporters. Why? Because the attitude of people who are chasing miracles is, "So what are you going to do for us this time?" Remember that the crowds ate Jesus' miraculous meal and the next day demanded a sign from Him.

Some years ago a physician who was curious about so-called faith healers and their amazing claims decided to find out for himself if there was anything to it. He volunteered to serve as an usher at a well-known faith healer's crusade, without revealing his identity or purpose.

This man did not profess to be a Christian, and his purpose was strictly investigative. He helped people in wheelchairs and on crutches come onto the stage for their healing and watched as they were pronounced healed. He obtained the names and addresses of these people and followed up on some of the cases afterward. He found that the people had not really been healed at all. He wrote about his experiences, and it is quite possible that some people who read his report felt justified in not believing in Jesus. I want to be perfectly clear here. I do believe that Jesus heals authentically. My own testimony is that I believe He has supernaturally healed me on several occasions. I am not at all dismissing or denigrating the healing power of Jesus. I am trying to get things into perspective.

If I spent my ministry laying hands on people and telling them they were healed, I'd be a little afraid to have a doctor follow up on my work. But I don't have to be afraid that anyone who comes to the cross and truly believes will go away the same as he came.

Someone might say, "You're just making excuses because you can't lay your hands on people and heal them." No, I don't need to make excuses. The apostles performed miracles of healing in Acts, but they did not take to the road as healers. Jesus said that there was no one born of woman who was greater than John the Baptist (Matthew 11:11). But we are told in John 10:41 that "John [the Baptist] did no miracle." The word is singular there. John did not do even one miracle.

But look at what follows that comment. "All things that John spake of this man [Jesus] were true. And many believed on him there" (vv. 41-42). I would rather have the gift that John the Baptist had than the supernatural ability to do miracles. What was John's message about Jesus? We've run into it again and again. "Behold the Lamb of God, which taketh away the sin of the world."

All God had to do to create the universe was speak the word, and it was so. The only time God had trouble was at bloody Calvary. To heal a crippled child is no difficulty to God, if that's what He wishes to do. But to save a soul requires the blood and agony of Calvary. Behold the wisdom and the power of God at the cross.

THE CROSS IS GOD'S SUPREME WORD OF CONDEMNATION

If the world does not understand anything else about the cross, the world needs to understand that the cross is God's supreme word of condemnation to those who do not believe. Paul called those who dismissed the cross as foolishness "them that perish" (1 Corinthians 1:18).

The cross of Jesus Christ was a judgment—not of Him, but of the human race. Jesus' crucifiers thought they were condemning Him, but in nailing Him to the cross they condemned themselves. We saw in a previous chapter that it pleased God the Father to send His beloved Son to the cross to pay the price for our sins. But we can never forget that the sin of wicked men also nailed Jesus to the cross.

Anyone who scoffs at the seriousness of sin needs to look at the cross. Anyone who doubts or denies the power of sin to condemn needs to look at the cross. What sin did to Jesus Christ, our substitute, in His humanity is an illustration of what sin will do to us if we refuse to believe in Him.

Sin was judged fully and finally at the cross, and there is no other remedy. Anyone who rejects Jesus has nothing else to look forward to except "a certain fearful looking for of judgment and fiery indignation, which shall devour [God's] adversaries" (Hebrews 10:27). And then as if to punctuate his point, the writer of Hebrews added, "It is a fearful thing to fall into the hands of the living God" (v. 31).

We live in a culture that doesn't like to believe in sin. We want to excuse or deny or minimize it, but the cross strips away all the veneers we try to add to hide sin. When we see Jesus Christ on the cross as our substitute, it reveals God's holy horror of sin. Written across the bleeding, broken body of Jesus as He became our sin-bearer is God's word of judgment: "The soul that sinneth, it shall die" (Ezekiel 18:20).

The cross speaks of the power, the presence, and the penalty of sin. It is God's supreme word of condemnation on those who refuse to come to Jesus and be saved.

Now we know that not all of those who are perishing realize the eternal danger they are in. Many people who are without Jesus Christ would say, "What do you mean I'm perishing? I don't see any problem. I'm having a good time."

In 2003 I clipped an article from the newspaper about Playboy founder Hugh Hefner on the fiftieth anniversary of his pornographic empire. The writer who interviewed Hefner was an unabashed admirer of "Hef," admitting that he was a collector of the magazine and had every issue ever published.

Hefner, who was seventy-seven when the article was published, announced with great glee, "We all now live in a playboy world." Hefner went on to say that the esteemed newspaper columnist George Will told him, "You won." That is, Hefner set out fifty years ago to lead a sexual revolution in America, and Will had to admit that Hefner had achieved his aim.

So in this interview Hugh Hefner was gloating in his triumph. He said it was nice to have all the battles with the moralists over and to live long enough to see the "victory" of the filth and adultery he had promoted (my terminology). The writer of the article clearly agreed with Hefner and lauded him for his victorious struggle against the "pleasure police."

Here was a man in his silk robe in his Playboy mansion, surrounded by a bevy of young beauties, the envy of many—and yet according to the Bible he is perishing. But he doesn't think he's perishing. He thinks he's doing fine. He's saying, "I won! I set out to change America, and I did it."

I hope Hugh Hefner will repent and get saved. God loves him. But until he, or anyone else who is lost, is willing to come and bow at the foot of the cross, the cross will remain a word of judgment and condemnation. That final judgment is sure, but yet to come. One day the warm flames of lust will turn into the fiery flames of hell.

The Cross Is God's Supreme Word of Justification

I am so glad the Bible doesn't put a period on a sentence before it's time. The first half of 1 Corinthians 1:18 speaks of judgment, but then we read, "But unto us which are saved [the cross] is the power of God."

One of the most amazing examples of the power of the cross to save was the thief hanging next to Jesus. This man repented of his accusations earlier in the day and pled simply, "Lord, remember me when thou comest into thy kingdom" (Luke 23:42). Jesus' answer was a word of salvation: "Verily I say unto thee, To day shalt thou be with me in paradise" (v. 43).

On the cross Jesus became my substitute and yours. We argued at the very outset of this book that the death of Christ was a substitutionary atonement. Jesus died not just on my behalf but in my place.

The world doesn't like the idea of substitution. The world does not like a blood sacrifice. As we said above, it is offensive to upstanding, educated, cultured people that their only hope for eternity is the blood of Jesus shed on the cross. The world believes in education rather than regeneration. The world prefers culture to Calvary. But the word of God is true: "There is none other name under heaven given among men, whereby we must be saved" (Acts 4:12).

It is very interesting to read John 3 and 4 together, the stories of Nicodemus and the woman at the well. Nicodemus was a respected leader and teacher in Israel, at the top of the social and religious ladder. The woman at the well was a hated, half-breed Samaritan who was a five-time loser in marriage. But both Nicodemus and this woman needed to be saved, and saved in exactly the same way.

I have often said there is no one too good to be saved and no one too bad to be saved. It was reported that Queen Victoria once came to hear the great evangelist Dwight L. Moody preach as Moody and his song leader, Ira Sankey, turned Great Britain upside down. The queen had heard of Moody's fame and wanted to see and hear for herself what all the commotion was about. Moody preached his usual straightforward message of sin and salvation through the finished work of Christ on the cross, and people flocked forward to be saved.

Afterward Queen Victoria was asked what she thought of the service. "It is not the kind of religious excitement that I prefer," she replied. But she went on to say that it was fine for those who enjoyed that sort of thing.

Moody had poor grammar, which turned off a lot of educated people, and a rough-and-tumble style that was necessary in his work with young street toughs, drunks, and down-and-outers in Chicago. But praise God that Dwight Moody did not alter his message for the queen or anyone else.

THE CROSS IS GOD'S SUPREME WORD OF SANCTIFICATION

Here is our final point of the chapter, and for this I want us to focus on one small phrase in 1 Corinthians 1:18: "Unto us *which are saved* [the cross] is the power of God" (emphasis added).

I hope you're coming to appreciate the richness and expressiveness of the Greek language. Here is another very wonderful example. The phrase "which are saved" can be translated "which are being saved." This is the present tense of the verb, speaking of continuous action. We are being saved every second of our lives by the power of God. This process is called sanctification, or becoming more like Christ.

We're used to hearing someone say, "I was saved when I was nineteen" or "I've been saved for forty years." I came to Christ over half a century ago, but I wonder what would happen if I stood up in church one day and said, "Praise God, He saved me yesterday" or "I am trusting God to save me tomorrow and next week too."

I'm sure I would get some funny looks, but that's what it means to be saved by the power of the cross. That's because salvation comes in three tenses. I was saved the day I trusted Christ as a teenager, I'm being saved and kept every day, and I will be saved when Jesus returns or I go to be with Him. I have been saved from the penalty of sin, which is justification. I am being saved from the power of sin, which is sanctification. And praise the Lord, someday I will be saved from the presence of sin, which is glorification.

In Philippians 1:6 Paul wrote, "Being confident of this very thing, that he which hath begun a good work in you will perform it until the day of Jesus Christ." That covers our salvation from the day we believe until we are in heaven. The cross is

God's power to save me day by day—and I need to be saved daily from myself, from sin, and from Satan.

How does the cross sanctify us? Jesus explained it when He said, "Whoever will come after me, let him deny himself, and take up his cross, and follow me" (Mark 8:34). People say, "Well, I guess this lumbago is my cross to bear," or "My spouse is my cross."

No, your cross is not a somebody or a something. And neither is your cross something you just carry around wherever you go. No, no. When a person put a cross upon his back, he was on his way to die. Jesus carried His cross to Calvary.

When Jesus says, "Take up your cross and follow Me," He means that we are to go to Calvary with Him to die, to take death upon ourselves, to be crucified with Christ. Your cross is not something that happens to you. Your cross is something you take up. It's a death you volunteer for.

Now because Jesus suffered and died on the cross of Calvary, we do not have to hang on a cross to pay for our sins. But we are called to "die daily" (1 Corinthians 15:31) to ourselves and our desires, plans, and ambitions. The cross sanctifies us by teaching us to say no to the flesh and yes to God, just as Jesus Christ did when He willingly drank from the cup of suffering that His Father had for Him.

When you can say each day, "Lord Jesus, I want to willingly and gladly say no to myself and yes to You. I choose the Calvary road. Help me to follow You whatever it takes and wherever You lead me," then you will discover an incredible power at work in your life—the power of the cross. The world may think the cross is a foolish and weak way to live, but let us who know Christ learn to live in its power.

8

The Silence of the Lamb

Dr. Ravi Zacharias is a Christian lecturer and apologist who has spoken on the campuses of literally dozens of prestigious universities here in America and other parts of the world. Going right into the heart of postmodern, irreligious academia with a clear message about Christ, Dr. Zacharias has encountered more than his share of noisy crowds and people loudly protesting his message.

But he said recently that during the last twenty minutes of his typical two-day presentation, when he talks about the cross and what Jesus Christ did there to ransom mankind and give us hope, there is silence. Dr. Zacharias said it doesn't matter which university he is visiting because the reaction is generally the same. The room or lecture hall often becomes so quiet when he is talking about Jesus and the cross that you can hear the proverbial pin drop. Dr. Zacharias said the reason for this is that people are deeply hungry for reality and hope.

I find it fascinating that the message of the cross can reduce a large audience to silence, because silence is actually one of the prominent themes we can trace through the passion of Jesus

Christ. An old spiritual about the death of Jesus says that even though He was perfectly innocent and did not deserve to die, "He never said a mumblin' word" either in protest of His unfair treatment or to defend Himself. We need to learn why Jesus stood before His accusers and crucifiers and "opened not his mouth" (Isaiah 53:7) and what the silence of the Lamb of God means for us.

How different Jesus' response at His trials and crucifixion is from ordinary human nature. Even when we have done something wrong and know we are wrong, still the first words that tend to form in our mouths are words of excuse and self-defense.

And what about when we are right but are blamed for being wrong? Most of us would be quick to speak up and protest our innocence. It's just human nature to want to speak up and justify ourselves.

But Jesus met His accusers with silence, even as the prophet Isaiah wrote seven hundred years before the fact. Isaiah 53:7 continues, "He is brought as a lamb to the slaughter, and as a sheep before her shearers is dumb, so he openeth not His mouth."

How does a lamb respond to its executioner? With meekness and submission. Here is a picture of the Lord Jesus Christ, who was and is absolutely sinless, being unjustly accused and yet offering no defense or excuse whatsoever. There was no protest from His lips as He was slandered, and He made no effort to avoid the false accusations and the cross that would follow.

This is true even though the trials Jesus endured—and there were about six altogether—were held illegally and were a mockery of justice. It was crass, coldhearted sin that judged Jesus guilty and brought Him to the cross. The interesting thing is that Jesus never protested or sought to justify Himself. He was silent in the face of His accusers. This facet of His passion and death leads to a great lesson for our lives and a great blessing for our hearts.

JESUS DID NOT OFFER A WORD OF SELF-DEFENSE AT HIS TRIALS

Over and over again the Bible records the silence of God's Lamb in the presence of His accusers. We read in Matthew 26 concerning Jesus' middle-of-the-night trial at the palace of the Jewish high priest, Caiaphas: "The high priest arose, and said unto him, Answerest thou nothing? what is it which these witness against thee? But Jesus held his peace" (vv. 62-63a; see also Mark 14:60-61). This is amazing, especially given that the witnesses hurling charges against Jesus were giving false testimony (Matthew 26:59-61).

Jesus Chose to Be Silent and Bear the Accusations

Now let me say that when we talk about the silence of Jesus during His passion, we are not saying that He never uttered one word at any point in any of His trials. In Matthew 26 the high priest finally said, "I adjure thee by the living God, that thou tell us whether thou be the Christ, the Son of God. Jesus saith unto him, Thou hast said" (vv. 63b-64a).

What Caiaphas did here was to put Jesus under oath before God, and so He was obliged to answer. Jesus could not and did not deny who He is. But this was not an act of self-defense or self-justification in the face of false witnesses. It was simply the truth. So the point is still made that the Lord Jesus offered no explanation for His actions or the charges made against Him.

We see a similar reaction in John 18:33 when Pilate asked Jesus during their private conversation, "Art thou the King of the Jews?" Jesus answered Pilate with a question of His own because Pilate needed to see the truth. So the Roman governor pressed on: "Art thou a king then? Jesus answered, Thou sayest that I am a king" (v. 37). But notice again that there is nothing in the way of excuse or defense in this exchange. The fact is that Pilate was on trial in his questioning of Jesus, and Jesus wanted Pilate to realize that fact.

But when it came to those who accused and blasphemed Jesus, the Bible records at the same trial: "When he was accused of the chief priests and elders, he answered nothing. Then said Pilate unto him, Hearest thou not how many things they witness against thee? And he answered him to never a word; insomuch that the governor marveled greatly" (Matthew 27:12-14; see also Mark 15:1-5).

Jesus also appeared before King Herod, who had heard about this miracle-worker and wanted to see Jesus do His stuff. Herod tried to make Jesus perform like a court jester, but the Savior greeted Herod's taunts with the disdain and silence they deserved. According to Luke 23:9-10: "Then [Herod] questioned with him in many words; but he answered him nothing. And the chief priests and scribes stood and vehemently accused him."

Let me give you one more telling example of Jesus' silence. After Pilate had finished examining Jesus and had made his decision against the truth, he compounded his sin by having the Lord scourged and beaten. But then the Jews scared Pilate by saying that Jesus deserved death because He had claimed to be the Son of God. In great fear, Pilate ran back into the judgment hall and asked Jesus, "Whence art thou?" (John 19:9). But the Bible says, "Jesus gave him no answer," because He had nothing left to say to Pilate. This pandering Roman politician had already turned a blind eye to the truth.

When we read these Scriptures, we wonder why Jesus did not say something to vindicate Himself. Again, it is the natural tendency of our human flesh to justify ourselves when we are guilty—and even more so when we are innocent and are being falsely accused.

Jesus Had to Be Silent to Fully Bear Our Sins

Why was the dear Savior so silent? I believe we find at least part of the answer in the great prophecy of Isaiah 53: "Surely he hath borne our griefs, and carried our sorrows: yet we did esteem him stricken, smitten of God, and afflicted. But he was wounded for our transgressions, he was bruised for our iniquities: the chastisement of our peace was upon him; and with his stripes we are healed. All we like sheep have gone astray; we have turned every one to his own way; and the LORD hath laid on him the iniquity of us all" (vv. 4-6).

Going on to verse 10, we read: "Yet it pleased the LORD to bruise him; he hath put him to grief: when thou shalt make his soul an offering for sin, he shall see his seed, he shall prolong his days, and the pleasure of the LORD shall prosper in his hand." The apostle Paul put it this way: "For he hath made him to be sin for us, who knew no sin; that we might be made the righteousness of God in him" (2 Corinthians 5:21).

Jesus' Shame Means Salvation for Us

The Bible teaches us that when Jesus Christ took our sin, He took all of the punishment that goes with that sin. A part of that punishment is shame. Had Jesus defended Himself and protested His innocence, He would have suffered no shame, and that would have left us guilty.

Jesus could not prove Himself innocent and then die in our place the shameful death that we deserve. Thank God that Jesus was willing to be counted a sinner before God, that we might be counted as righteous before God!

Jesus held back any words that would have relieved Him from the shame and blame of sin. He was not a sinner, but He took fully the sinner's place.

And here's another thought to consider. If Jesus had risen up in His own defense during His trials, I believe that He would have been so powerful and irrefutable in making His defense that no governor, high priest, or other legal authority on earth could have stood against Him!

In other words, if Jesus had taken up His own defense with the intention of refuting His accusers and proving His innocence, He would have won! But we would have lost, and we would be lost for all eternity.

And even if He chose not to act as His own defense attorney, Jesus still had limitless power to protect Himself. Jesus was so powerful that those who came to Gethsemane to arrest Him shrank back and fell to the ground like dead men when Jesus simply said, "I am he" (John 18:5-6). Had Jesus wanted to, He could have spoken them all into oblivion.

Remember that Jesus withered a fig tree with a word (Mark 11:14). He could just as easily have withered the hand that held the whip or the hammer. And beyond all of that, He told Peter in the garden to put away his sword, saying, "Thinkest thou that I cannot now pray to my Father, and he shall presently give me more than twelve legions of angels?" (Matthew 26:53).

Now, the Bible records that just one angel of God once slew 185,000 men (2 Kings 19:35). Twelve legions of angels would be at least 144,000 angels. So if Jesus called that many angels with that kind of power, you can do the math and see that the Savior could have surrounded Himself with an invincible army. And every angel would have lined up for duty, for we can be sure that the hosts of heaven were leaning over the battlements of glory during Jesus' passion and death, ready for the word to come to His side. But Jesus never issued the call because He came to die for our sins.

They accused Jesus of blasphemy, lying, sedition, and many other things, but the Savior answered not a word. This is the amazing silence of the Lamb.

SINNERS WILL NOT HAVE A WORD OF SELF-DEFENSE AT THE JUDGMENT

Since Jesus took our place on the cross as God's only remedy for sin, those who refuse to trust Him as Savior, to put their faith where God has put their sins, will find themselves speechless when they stand before a holy God.

In Romans 3 God brings at least fourteen telling indictments against the whole human race and then gives this summation as a prosecutor would do after presenting his case: "Now we know that what things soever the law saith, it saith to them who are under the law: that every mouth may be stopped, and all the world may become guilty before God" (v. 19).

A time is coming when every guilty mouth will be stopped. No sinful son or daughter of Adam will be able to offer a word of excuse, defense, or justification at the Great White Throne judgment seat of God (Revelation 20:11-15). When God opens His books, every mouth will close.

The Silence of the Lost Will Mean Condemnation Someday

The silence of the Lamb means salvation, but the silence of the lost means condemnation. The silence of the Lamb is, for us, joyous, but the silence of the lost is ominous.

We all know there are times when silence can indeed be ominous. A retired guard at the infamous Attica State Prison in New York described a time like this as he told of the tense atmosphere in the prison in the days and weeks leading up to the bloody riot in 1971—the deadliest prison uprising in U.S. history.

This guard said that the very day before the riot broke out, a group of over five hundred prisoners filed into the massive dining hall for a meal. But instead of getting their trays and sitting down to eat, the inmates simply stood in rows behind the tables with their heads bowed—not in prayer but in defiance. Not a word was spoken. The guard said a complete, eerie silence descended over the huge hall as these prisoners, to a man, stood in quiet protest without a sound being heard.

To this former Attica guard, the sight of those inmates was a frightening sign of things to come. "The reason it scared us is that we knew the inmates had gotten together and organized themselves. And we knew that if the inmates had organized, something bad was about to happen."

Sure enough, the siege of Attica began the next day and ended days later with over thirty inmates and ten hostages dead. Most of the hostages had been shot by the state police who assaulted the prison to retake it.

The Bible says that those whose names are not found in the Book of Life because they refused Christ will stand before God at the last judgment in utter silence with their heads bowed, just like those prisoners. But on that day there will be no rebellion against authority; the only sound will be God's word of condemnation: "I never knew you: depart from me, ye that work iniquity" (Matthew 7:23).

Now Is the Time for the Lost to Be Silent

How much better it would be for guilty sinners if they would put their hands over their mouths here on earth, accept God's verdict that "all have sinned" (Romans 3:23), and turn to Christ while there is time. But our human propensity for self-justification keeps coming to the fore.

Some have said that from a literary standpoint, Jesus' parable of the Good Samaritan is the most perfect story ever told. But let us remember that the occasion that prompted this story was the attempt of an expert in the Jewish law to cover himself when Jesus told him to love his neighbor.

"But he [the lawyer], willing to *justify himself*, said unto Jesus, And who is my neighbour?" (Luke 10:29, emphasis added). This lawyer was looking for a loophole in the law because he did not truly want to love all people. He would have been much better off simply to take Jesus' exhortation to heart and practice it rather than opening his mouth to challenge the Lord.

We all want to justify ourselves. A drunkard says, "I drink because my wife nags me." His wife says, "I nag him because he drinks." Eve said the devil had beguiled her. Adam said he sinned because of the woman God had given him.

Do you know what an excuse is? That's what someone else says to defend his behavior. But when *we* do it, we call it a reason because that sounds much better. But whether excuse or reason, it doesn't matter when people stand before God, for the time is coming when the unsaved sinner will stand before the Great White Throne and all excuses will falter and fail.

Jesus once depicted this truth in the parable of the wedding feast (Matthew 22:1-14). When all the guests were assembled in the wedding hall, the king who was hosting the wedding saw a guest without a wedding garment. "And he saith unto him, Friend, how camest thou in hither not having a wedding garment? And he was speechless. Then said the king to the servants, Bind him hand and foot, and take him away, and cast him into outer darkness; there shall be weeping and gnashing of teeth" (vv. 12-13).

In this parable the king represents God the Father, and the son getting married typifies the Lord Jesus Christ. The wedding feast typifies salvation. At such a wedding, the host would provide wedding garments without any cost to those who came. A servant would meet the guests at the door with a wedding garment. Anyone who was foolish enough to try and crash the wedding without the proper garment was guilty and therefore speechless when confronted by the host. It would have done the man in the parable no good to protest, "I have no garment" or "You mean I'm not fit for the king dressed as I am?"

Jesus made it clear that the man was not acceptable, and that man knew it. He had nothing to say as he was consigned to outer darkness, a terrible picture of hell.

No sinner will ever know true salvation until his mouth of self-justification is stopped, he pleads guilty before God, and he receives Christ as his Savior (Romans 3:19).

SAINTS WILL NOT HEAR A WORD OF CONDEMNATION AT THE JUDGMENT

The silence of the lost means eternal judgment, but the Bible speaks of another silence that is golden indeed. This is the utter lack of condemnation that will be enjoyed by those who cast themselves at the foot of the cross and plead the blood of Jesus over their sins.

We Are Safe Forever in Jesus Christ

Isaiah's great prophecy of God's suffering and saving Lamb continues with these words: "He shall see of the travail of his soul, and shall be satisfied: by his knowledge shall my righteous servant justify many; for he shall bear their iniquities" (Isaiah 53:11.)

Thank God that He saw the travail of Jesus on the cross and counted His suffering as a satisfactory offering for sin. When we come to know Jesus, we don't need self-justification because He justifies us. And because we are justified, the Bible declares, "There is therefore now no condemnation to them which are in Christ Jesus" (Romans 8:1).

There will be not one word of condemnation for the saints of God at the judgment. Because Christ died in our place,

Almighty God will never raise a word of condemnation against a twice-born person. We could call this the silence of the Lord.

Earlier in Romans, Paul had written, "But to him that worketh not, but believeth on him that justifieth the ungodly, his faith is counted for righteousness. Even as David also describeth the blessedness of the man, unto whom God imputeth righteousness without works, Saying, Blessed are they whose iniquities are forgiven, and whose sins are covered. Blessed is the man to whom the Lord will not impute sin" (Romans 4:5-8).

This Scripture is almost too marvelous to believe. Think of what it teaches. One: Our iniquities are forgiven—all of them. We are sinners by birth, sinners by nature, and sinners by practice. But those iniquities are forgiven!

Two: Our sins are blotted out. Every stain, every blur, every blot, every blemish is covered by the precious blood of Christ. "Though your sins be as scarlet, they will be white as snow" (Isaiah 1:18).

Three: Righteousness is imputed to us. This means that the righteousness of Christ is credited to our account. And by the way, His righteousness is the only garment that will admit us to the wedding supper of the Lamb (Revelation 19:7-10).

Imagine what it would be like to have every voice speaking against you silenced. God Himself will stop every such voice that tries. "Who shall lay any thing to the charge of God's elect? It is God that justifieth. Who is he that condemneth? It is Christ that died, yea rather, that is risen again, who is even at the right hand of God, who also maketh intercession for us" (Romans 8:33-34).

First John 2:1 says that Jesus is our Advocate, our defense attorney, before the Father. Many will try to condemn us, but God will not allow it. If one word of condemnation were ever to come from Almighty God, then we would be cast into hell. But thank God, it will never come!

We Need to Speak Up in Praise of Jesus Christ

What does all of this mean as we consider the silence of the Lamb and His justification for each of us?

First, because Jesus was silent, I should never be silent when it comes to my witness for Him. How can I be ashamed of the One who took all of my shame? My prayer is that God will help all believers to be bold verbal witnesses for the Lamb who died without opening His mouth.

Second, for Jesus' shame in bearing my sins on the cross, I will give Him glory. I want to say with David, "I will bless the LORD at all times: his praise shall continually be in my mouth" (Psalm 34:1). It is unthinkable that we could be redeemed by such love and yet not praise God forever and ever.

My dear wife, Joyce, has written a wonderful piece of prose about the silence of God's Lamb.

NEVER A WORD

Jesus stood before Pilate;
His accusers stood near by;
They agreed together to tell
many things that were not so.
But He answered nothing!

Pilate asked, "Why don't You answer;
Don't You hear all the things
they're saying?"
Pilate marveled that
still Jesus answered nothing!

The soldiers then took Jesus
To the judgment hall—
They stripped Him
and robed Him;
They pressed a crown
of thorns into His brow;
They mocked Him and
spat on Him—

hailed Him as
"King of the Jews."
They reviled Him, but—
He reviled not!

He was brought as a lamb
to the slaughter—
Spotless and perfect Lamb of God.
But as a sheep who protests
not before her shearers,
so this Lamb opened not
His mouth!

Pilate marveled greatly that
He answered not a word!
I, too, can only marvel at this
Godlike kind of love.

How unlike the Savior I
seem to always be—
With many words I protest and
claim my innocence.

"Oh, make me into Thy likeness!"

I will never comprehend the
Savior's love for me;
that never a word came in defense.
He could not explain;
They could not understand—
Though sinless,
He was guilty!

My sins were upon Him;
I deserved the mocking,
the scourging,
the awful pain,
but He bore it all
and answered
never a word!

PART III

CHRIST'S PURPOSE
FOR US
IN HIS PASSION

9

SAY GOOD-BYE TO BOASTING

Boasting in any form is offensive to God. And as much as we would like to think that all the proud, self-inflated people are outside the church, that simply isn't true. Prideful, man-made religion is all around us. The secular humanists declared in their manifesto that we cannot wait around for God to come and save the human race. Prideful religionists say they are just the ones God has been waiting around for because they are so good!

The problem with a lot of man-made religion is that those who practice it are measuring themselves by the wrong standard. Paul wrote to the prideful church in Corinth about those who "measur[e] themselves by themselves, and compar[e] themselves among themselves" (2 Corinthians 10:12). We can always find somebody worse than ourselves to measure ourselves against, and when we do that we come away looking pretty good—or so we think.

But the standard we as believers are called to follow is not each other, but Jesus and Him crucified. It is at the cross of

Christ that we see ourselves and our sins in all their ugliness. In Galatians 6:14 Paul set the true standard for our self-evaluation: "God forbid that I should glory, save in the cross of our Lord Jesus Christ."

I trust that we have established the centrality of the cross in Christ's passion. Therefore, I want to spend the final two chapters of this book dealing with the question of Christ's purpose for us in His passion. That is, having seen Jesus on the cross, how are we now to live?

That's worth a whole book in itself, but we are going to limit ourselves to what I believe are two fundamental attitudes we need to adopt.

I want us to see first of all that the cross excludes human pride. The Bible says, "For by grace are ye saved through faith; and that not of yourselves: it is the gift of God: not of works, lest any man should boast" (Ephesians 2:8-9). "While we were yet sinners, Christ died for us" (Romans 5:8). "For I know that in me (that is, in my flesh,) dwelleth no good thing" (Romans 7:18). The stark reality of our unworthiness before God leads us to ask, as did Paul, "Where is boasting then? It is excluded . . . by the law of faith" (Romans 3:27). Let's consider three truths that demonstrate this fact.

BOASTING IS EXCLUDED BY THE METHOD OF GOD'S SALVATION

The reason the apostle Paul said all boasting is sinful apart from the cross is that the cross of Christ is the only means of salvation. Salvation is in the cross alone, by grace alone, through faith alone, in Christ alone. We come back to Paul's declaration, "It pleased God by the foolishness of preaching to save them that believe" (1 Corinthians 1:21).

The Cross Shows Man's Total Unworthiness for Salvation

How does the preaching of the cross strike a fatal blow to human pride? First of all, it shows our total unworthiness to receive the grace of God. When you tell people that there is nothing they can do to save themselves and that they are going to have to be saved by the crucified Christ and the blood of the cross alone, that leaves no room for pride. And that is a thorn in the side of many people today.

Have you ever noticed how much of modern marketing and advertising is built around the idea of what people deserve? We were told by a popular hamburger chain, "You deserve a break today." Models tell us that the products they are selling are the most expensive or luxurious items available, "but you're worth it." We are also constantly reminded, "You owe it to yourself" or "You have this coming to you."

The same thing is true in so much religious advertising and preaching today. People are told that Jesus is waiting to solve their confusion or loneliness or lack of purpose. But these things are totally apart from the issue of salvation. The human dilemma is not what sin has done to us in making us lonely or unhappy, but the offense that sin is against the holiness of God. Sin is an affront to God, a clenched fist in His face.

Many "seeker-friendly" ministries tell us you can't attract people to the church by talking about sin and the cross and how bad off they are without Christ. But I don't find in the Bible that God has done a widening project on the narrow road that leads to salvation. That road starts at Calvary, and at Calvary human pride is laid in the dust.

What I'm saying is that in God's sight, we deserve nothing but judgment. If we don't understand that, we will never have a sense of gratitude to God. If we think we richly deserve what we are about to get, we will not feel grateful when we get it. It's more likely that we will feel very self-satisfied—or perhaps even angry if somebody got more than we did.

The Cross Shows Man's Complete Inability to Save Himself

Ask some people why they think they are going to heaven and you will get a grocery list of their good qualities and good deeds. But the old hymn has it right: "Nothing in my hand I bring; simply to thy cross I cling."

One of my favorite stories is of a little boy who came forward in church professing his faith in Christ. The counselor asked him if he was saved, and the boy replied that he was. "I did my part, and God did His part, and now I'm saved."

This didn't sound right to the counselor, so he asked the boy to explain. "I did the sinning, and God did the saving." He got it right. That's the gospel.

One of our problems today is that we have become too smart and sophisticated to believe the message of the cross. I would invite you to review our discussion of 1 Corinthians 1:18ff. in Chapter 7 to remind yourself of God's opinion of human wisdom. We have more knowledge today than we have ever had. Yesterday's fanciful science fiction is today's technology. And yet we are in greater danger than we have ever been.

On a recent trip I looked around at the people sitting near me at the airport. Across the way was a man working on a laptop computer. On his right and left were people talking on cell phones. Down at the end of the row was another person with a laptop, and someone else was working on a Palm Pilot. And there I was with a pencil and a yellow legal pad! It was amazing to see all these products in use.

We are in a technological transition now that is absolutely

without precedent. It is coming at us so fast, it's like drinking from a fire hose. I drive a computer-operated automobile. My dashboard tells me if I'm running out of gas, the door isn't shut, or the trunk lid is open.

If I want to transmit a message to my secretary, neither of us has to be in the office. I can pick up a phone and dictate to her answering machine while I'm driving. Then when I get home, I can heat my tea in a few seconds and sit with a remote in my hand watching news reports from all over the world.

There is no question that we are smarter than we've ever been, but we are not wiser. And human wisdom will never lead us to God. He counts it as foolishness because it leads us away from the cross.

BOASTING IS EXCLUDED BY THE MAKEUP OF GOD'S SAINTS

We also discover that we have nothing to brag about when we realize that God has largely bypassed those whom the world considers to be really important.

> *For ye see your calling, brethren, how that not many wise men after the flesh, not many mighty, not many noble, are called: But God hath chosen the foolish things of the world to confound the wise; and God hath chosen the weak things of the world to confound the things which are mighty; and base things of the world, and things which are despised, hath God chosen, yea, and things which are not, to bring to nought things that are: that no flesh should glory in his presence. (1 Corinthians 1:26-29)*

Not only is the *message* of the cross a blow to human pride, but the *messengers* whom God frequently uses to tell the story are also a blow to human pride.

For too long the church has been plagued by our fascination

with the high and mighty and famous of this world. A lot of us believe that if we can just get the movers and shakers into the church, then we'll get somewhere and gain some stature in the world.

Now don't get me wrong. We need to share the gospel with people in all strata of society, from the up-and-inners to the down-and-outers. But the Bible says that very few of the world's elite have ever come to humble themselves at the cross. God chooses what the world considers foolish people to deliver what the world calls a foolish message. The Greek word for "foolish" is *moros*, from which we get our word *moron*.

Now don't be offended by that. Paul was just referring to those who are not necessarily Phi Beta Kappas or Ph.Ds. If you are, I am glad for you. And I have some good news—God can use you too. He will have to work a little harder to do it, but He can. I say that somewhat lightheartedly, but seriously you are in the minority in the body of Christ, for the rest of us are pretty common people.

Abraham Lincoln once said that God must love ordinary-looking people because He made so many of them. I'd like to paraphrase that and say that God must love to use ordinary people because He uses so many of them.

I mentioned D. L. Moody in an earlier chapter. Although he was a man of enormous energy and "street smarts," Moody was a fifth-grade dropout who was said to murder the English language. A man once told Moody that he was offended by his grammar. Moody knew the man, so he asked him, "And how many people have you won to Christ with your grammar?"

Moody also rode his pony through the streets of Chicago, handing out candy to draw street kids to his Sunday school. He was known in his early days as "Crazy Moody." But God used him to shake two continents. Moody was so well known in Chicago for his zeal for Christ that one time, when he asked a man on the street about his soul, the man retorted, "That's none of your business."

"Oh, yes, it is," Moody responded.

"Then you must be Moody."

I think also of Billy Sunday, the Billy Graham of the early part of the twentieth century. Billy Sunday was a former Major League baseball player who did some strange things at his crusades. He would slide across the stage to illustrate how we need to reach heaven. Many people considered Sunday to be an eccentric crank. His own biographer called him God's joke on the ministry. But God used Billy Sunday in a wonderful way because He delights to use intellectually common folk.

God also chooses the physically weak to confound the powerful and do His work. When I was pastoring in Florida, we had a special sports outreach week that included Paul Anderson, who was at that time the world's strongest man. He had a wonderful testimony for Christ. His testimony was essentially this: If the strongest man in the world needs Jesus, so do you.

But there was also a time of free testimony. A man who was a paraplegic was wheeled forward in his wheelchair. Friends lifted him to the platform. He was anything but an athlete. He gave a testimony, however, about what Jesus Christ meant to him. His face seemed to shine like the noonday sun.

The next Sunday in our church, a young man came forward to profess his faith in Christ. I asked him when he had been saved. He said, "During the Week of Champions."

I asked him, "Which night?"

"The night Paul Anderson spoke," he replied.

I asked him, "What was it about Paul Anderson's testimony that convicted you?"

His reply was wonderful. "To be very frank, I hardly remember what Paul Anderson said. It was the testimony of the man in the wheelchair. When I saw what God had done for that young man, and how He had given him victory over circumstances beyond his control, I said to myself, 'If God can do that for him, perhaps He can do something for me.'"

I have never forgotten that occasion. In that room was the strongest man in the world, and yet God used a paraplegic in a wheelchair. Don't insult God by saying that He cannot use you.

God also uses those who are economically debased. The word "base" in 1 Corinthians 1:28 means ignoble, from the wrong side of the tracks, without a pedigree. Most of us in the family of God do not come from a long line of old-money ancestors. Many believers are not necessarily poor, but in terms of this world they are not those who have economic or social clout.

Paul also spoke in verse 28 of people who are not on the highest rungs of the social ladder. These are God's little people. They're not in the Who's Who of the world; they're the "Who's Not." There is a very sad story about a woman back in the early part of the twentieth century who was a member of the most elite society of her day. Her family was the upper part of the upper crust. She had a strict rule in her house that the servants were never to speak to her directly.

This woman had a small child who had fallen ill, and one night while she was hosting a large party in her home, her child died. The servants caring for the child were distraught, but as they talked among themselves they agreed that they dare not tell the mistress of the house for fear of what would happen to them if they broke her rule. So this poor rich woman went on with her party, not even knowing her infant had died.

I'm not saying that all of the prominent, wealthy, and powerful people of this world are like that. But this story illustrates why it is so hard for people with this mind-set to humble themselves and bow at the foot of the cross.

Now the Bible doesn't say that not any mighty or noble people are saved, just not *many*. I thank God for those in science, medicine, government, commerce, and other highly visible public areas who love Jesus. But they are not the majority in God's army. What He loves to do is take the message of a crucified Savior and use ordinary people to spread that message across the world and in the doing of that bring glory to Himself. Remember God's declaration that "no flesh should glory in his presence" (v. 29). He will not share His glory with another.

BOASTING IS EXCLUDED BY THE MANNER OF THE MESSENGERS

The message of God's salvation and the makeup of His saints reveal that boasting is out of place for the Christian. But consider now the manner of God's messengers. For this we go once again to Paul's first letter to the prideful church at Corinth. "And I, brethren, when I came to you, came not with excellency of speech or of wisdom, declaring unto you the testimony of God. For I determined not to know any thing among you, save Jesus Christ, and him crucified" (1 Corinthians 2:1).

Preaching Christ Takes the Focus Off of Self

Paul's message was Christ-centered. Someone may say that seems restrictive. But preaching Christ is no more limiting to us than swimming in the Atlantic Ocean would be limiting to a minnow.

Everything we preach has to flow from the cross. If our message does not begin at the cross and lead back to the cross, there is something wrong with it. Of course, Paul preached on many issues and topics related to the faith. But his point in saying this was that everything he said was related to the cross of Jesus Christ.

In our pastors' conferences on Monday mornings, various pastors come and preach to the others. One dear pastor from whom I have learned much was a black pastor known as

Brother Brown. He was a man of great wisdom, and I was eager to hear him preach. But he had not gotten far into his preaching when he made a statement that startled me. He said, "I don't preach theology."

I was sitting there thinking to myself, *That's a shame. You ought to preach theology.* But then he said something I will never forget. "I use theology—I preach Jesus."

What a great statement. I have repeated that around the world. That's what Paul was saying. "I don't want to know anything but Christ and him crucified."

Paul certainly had no confidence in the flesh. He continued by saying, "And I was with you in weakness, and in fear, and in much trembling. And my speech and my preaching was not with enticing words of man's wisdom, but in demonstration of the Spirit and of power: that your faith should not stand in the wisdom of men, but in the power of God" (1 Corinthians 2:3-5). Paul refused to be an intellectual or oratorical showboat, even though he had all the credentials to pull it off. He was afraid that people would put their faith in him rather than in God.

I heard Billy Graham say on one occasion, "I stay frightened." What did he mean by that? He meant that he didn't want to do anything that would cause people to follow him rather than follow Jesus Christ. Dr. Graham understands that any person who is in the public eye can be tempted to manipulate people and gain a popular following by saying what people want to hear and playing to the crowd. He was saying he wants to stay constantly on guard against that very powerful temptation.

Jesus Christ and Him Crucified Is Something to Boast About

The problem with preaching the wisdom of men rather than the cross of Christ is that anything I can talk you into, somebody else can talk you out of. Paul was not opposed to wisdom in the true sense of that word. "Howbeit we speak wisdom among them that are perfect: yet not the wisdom of this world, nor of the princes of this world, that come to nought: But we speak the wisdom of God in a mystery, even the hidden wisdom" (vv. 6-7).

Paul refused to huckster the gospel or to use his platform and abilities to gain a personal following. He refused to do anything that would take his or other people's focus off the cross. "Let the world think I am a fool," was Paul's attitude; "I am going to preach Jesus Christ."

Here's a passage of Scripture I encourage you to memorize and meditate on often. Speaking through the pen of the prophet Jeremiah, God said to His people, "Thus saith the LORD, Let not the wise man glory in his wisdom, neither let the mighty man glory in his might, let not the rich man glory in his riches: But let him that glorieth glory in this, that he understandeth and knoweth me, that I am the LORD which exercise loving-kindness, judgment, and righteousness, in the earth: for in these things I delight, saith the LORD" (Jeremiah 9:23-24).

If you want something to brag about, brag about Jesus and what He has done for you. Tell people that God loved the world so much that He put a cross between us and hell. Remind them that anyone who goes to hell will have to climb over the cross of Jesus Christ to get there.

We have a lot to brag about, and it's all found in the cross. God forbid that we should boast in anything except the cross of Jesus Christ.

10

IT'S TIME FOR SOME LIBERATED LIVING

Preachers were taught in preaching classes that until we help people understand how the truth we have presented impacts them where they are, and until we help them see what they should do in light of what they have been taught, the task of preaching is not completed.

Another name for this process of putting shoe leather on our faith is application. We began to do this in the previous chapter, and now I want to finish this book by showing you what the message of the cross means to you as a follower of Jesus Christ. I want to ask you several important questions to begin. Here they are:

Are you tired of being a slave to the world, the flesh, and the devil? Are you weary of trying and failing to live in the freedom and victory the Bible talks about, but which you can't seem to find? Are you ready to be set free from bondage to the old way of life so you can breathe free air as a child of God?

If the answer to these questions is yes, I have some very good news for you. You can be emancipated! In fact, your freedom is complete and has already been purchased, paid in full at the cross by the blood of Christ.

One of the great truths of the Christian life that many believers never fully grasp is that the One who gave Himself *for* us also gave Himself *to* us so that we would have the power to live a life of victory. Until you come to grips with this, you will not understand the full meaning of Christ's passion.

It would be terrible to continue living as a slave even after you've been set free because no one told you that you were free. But that is what happened to slaves in Texas during the Civil War. Abraham Lincoln had signed the Emancipation Proclamation in 1863, but word of it did not reach Texas until two years later. During that interim, Texas slaves were free people still living in bondage. A festival is held in Texas every year, called Juneteenth, to commemorate the wonderful occasion when slaves in Texas finally learned they were free.

But here's something just as tragic. Other slaves who did get the word about their freedom still chose to stay on the plantation with their old masters because slavery was all they had ever known. They didn't know how to act as free people.

The Bible's emancipation proclamation for believers is found in Romans 6, a tremendous passage of Scripture that follows Paul's discussion of God's amazing grace that is greater than all our sin. In Romans 5:20 the apostle declared, "Where sin abounded, grace did much more abound." And then in chapter 6, he addressed the implications of that truth.

The first thing Paul wanted to make clear was that the superabounding nature of God's grace is not an excuse for us to sin or to live in defeat. "What shall we say then? Shall we continue in sin, that grace may abound? God forbid. How shall we, that are dead to sin, live any longer therein?" (vv. 1-2). Far from being an excuse for sin, grace is an inducement to live a righteous and a holy life. And grace also supplies the power to live such a life.

God forbid that any believer should be a slave to sin. God's will and plan for you is constant, conscious, and conspicuous victory.

Paul develops his thought in Romans 6 around three key words that I want to rivet into your heart and mind. These three words are *know*, *reckon*, and *yield*. These words deal with three corresponding concepts: *fact*, *faith*, and *function*. There is a fact to know, a reckoning to put your faith in, and a function as you yield to Christ. Let these words be etched upon your consciousness and the concepts behind them be fixed in your mind. Ask God to help you understand all that is involved in them.

YOU NEED TO *KNOW* SOMETHING TO ENJOY LIBERATED LIVING

The first word that Paul used in Romans 6 to convey his message is the word *know*. There is a very crucial and very wonderful fact you need to know about your salvation.

> *Knowing this, that our old man is crucified with him, that the body of sin might be destroyed, that henceforth we should not serve sin. For he that is dead is freed from sin. Now if we be dead with Christ, we believe that we shall also live with him: knowing that Christ being raised from the dead dieth no more; death hath no more dominion over him. For in that he died, he died unto sin once: but in that he liveth, he liveth unto God.* (vv. 6-10)

What is it that God wants you to know? He wants you to know that you are totally identified with Jesus Christ. This identity is so close that everything that happened to Jesus in His passion also happened to you. So when Jesus hung on the cross, you—that is, the old person you used to be—hung there too because Jesus was dying as your substitute. So you have become one with Jesus Christ in His death. Now, friend, you can't be the same after death as you were before you died! This transformation in a believer's identity is what the Bible means when it says that we are no longer in Adam but in Christ.

You Were Crucified with Christ

The cross had your name on it. This is important to understand because Calvary not only deals with the sin, but it also deals with the sinner. If all Jesus did was forgive my sin and not deal with me, He would not have delivered me from my worst enemy, which is myself and my sin nature. Galatians 2:20 explains what it means to be identified with Jesus in His death: "I am crucified with Christ: nevertheless, I live; yet not I, but Christ liveth in me." You were nailed to that cross with Jesus because He was taking your place.

I love to tell about the time one of the former pastors of our church, the great Dr. Robert G. Lee, visited Israel. He wanted to see Calvary more than anything. As Dr. Lee and his group stood at Calvary, their Israeli guide asked, "Have any of you ever been here before?" Dr. Lee raised his hand.

"When were you here?" the guide asked.

Dr. Lee replied, "Two thousand years ago." He understood the principle of his identification with Christ on the cross.

Now if our "old man," the person we used to be, was crucified with Christ, then we are free from sin. We still live in these old bodies, but sin does not have the power to hold us in its bondage any longer.

What happens to a convicted criminal who dies while awaiting transfer to the penitentiary to begin his sentence? That sentence doesn't apply anymore. It's irrelevant. The case is closed. The authorities can send that man's corpse to the penitentiary, or even to the execution chamber if they so choose, but it would be a waste of time. Even if the guilty man were found to be innocent after the fact and his conviction overturned, it wouldn't have any effect on him. Guilty or innocent, dead men are beyond human judgment.

A stern federal judge named Kennesaw Mountain Landis was chosen to clean up Major League baseball after the infamous "Black Sox" scandal of 1919. That year eight players on the Chicago White Sox conspired with gamblers and mobsters to throw the World Series to the Cincinnati Reds, an inferior team that everyone agreed could not have beaten the powerful White Sox in a legitimate series.

Judge Landis cleaned up the mess, banning all eight White Sox players from baseball for life in 1920 for taking part in the scheme. Several of the players fought furiously to get the judgment reversed so they could return to baseball, but to no avail. They never played another game in the Majors, and the ones who might otherwise have been elected to the Hall of Fame were also barred from that honor.

One of the so-called Black Sox was the legendary Shoeless Joe Jackson, an illiterate sharecropper's son whom many experts consider to be the greatest hitter of all time. Jackson insisted that he never received any money from the gamblers and that he had changed his mind and played his best in the 1919 World Series. Jackson begged to be reinstated, and many fans sympathized with him, believing that he had been talked into going along with the fix by the other players.

Now here's the interesting thing. Even though Joe Jackson died in 1951, there are still people today pleading with Major League baseball to lift Jackson's ban posthumously, clear his name, and allow him into the Baseball Hall of Fame.

If that ever happens, I can assure you that it will make no difference at all to Shoeless Joe Jackson. Dead men don't show up to their induction ceremonies to receive the applause and accolades of their fans.

You need to understand that since you have died with Christ, the old rules and the old relationships aren't in force anymore. That is especially true in regard to Satan. Because of Calvary you are no longer Satan's slave. The death of Jesus Christ changed all that.

You Were Buried with Christ

In chapter 3 of this book, we discussed the importance of our burial with Christ. But I want to review it briefly here so you can see this truth again in relation to the role it plays in victorious living.

Paul asked the Romans, "Know ye not, that so many of us as were baptized into Jesus Christ were baptized into his death? Therefore we are buried with him by baptism into death: that like as Christ was raised up from the dead by the glory of the Father, even so we also should walk in newness of life. For if we have been planted together in the likeness of his death, we shall also be in the likeness of his resurrection" (6:3-5).

You'll recall that Jesus' burial was important enough to be included in the gospel (1 Corinthians 15:3-4). Not only did Jesus' death have your name on it—His grave had your name on it too. Your "old man" that died with Jesus on the cross was buried with Him in Joseph of Arimathea's borrowed tomb.

Baptism symbolizes your burial with Christ. When you were baptized, you were buried in a liquid tomb, testifying that your sins are buried in the grave of God's forgetfulness. The devil would love to haunt you with the bones of your old life, but he has no authority to do that. When the devil tries to harass you, you need to say to him, "That old person you are looking for is dead. Didn't you hear? The funeral has already been held, and he's been put away."

Baptism is a believer's spiritual funeral. We are buried with Christ in baptism. That's the reason I believe in baptism by immersion. The Greek word *baptizo* means "to dip or immerse." Every time somebody goes into that watery grave of baptism, that pictures the glorious gospel of the Lord Jesus Christ.

You Were Raised with Christ

Praise God, you were also raised with Jesus Christ to "walk in newness of life." Just as we identify with Christ in His burial when we are baptized, so we identify with Him in His resurrection when we are brought up out of the water.

Aren't you glad you didn't stay under the waters of baptism? Jesus didn't stay in the grave, and neither did you. He has life that the grave cannot hold, and He has given that life to you! You are "a new creature" in Christ Jesus (2 Corinthians 5:17). And as this great verse goes on to say, "old things are passed away" for you. Remember that your baptism is only a figure or an illustration of our real death, burial, and resurrection in Jesus.

I sometimes use the imagery of a wax figure because I am reminded of a great story. A man I know once took his family to the Smithsonian Institution in Washington, D.C. They visited the section where the First Ladies of our country are represented by wax figures. This was back when Lyndon Johnson was President; so the new wax figure of his wife, Lady Byrd, was being featured.

My friend and his family were standing there looking at the incredibly lifelike wax figure of Lady Byrd Johnson when a woman came up to them and asked, "Well, how do you like it?"

They turned to look and couldn't believe their eyes. It was Mrs. Johnson herself, in the flesh. They had a nice conversation with her and took pictures. Lady Byrd was very nice to them, and my friend thought, *Wow! I can't believe this. Wait until we get home and tell people.*

While they were talking with the First Lady, a professional photographer came up and asked the group, "Would you mind stepping out of the way? I want to get a picture of Lady Bird."

So the wife of the President stepped aside while this photographer took a picture of her likeness in wax!

The devil would like to have you believe that the old you, your wax figure, is the real you. But you know better.

You may be saying, "OK, I know that. But if my 'old man' has been crucified and buried with Christ, why won't he lie still like the corpse he is? Why am I still having so much trouble with the old person I used to be?"

Perhaps it is because you haven't taken the next step. Knowing the truth is a necessary first step, but there is also something you need to *reckon* to be true.

You Need to *Reckon* Something to Enjoy Liberated Living

Reckoning has to do with appropriating all that Jesus has for you. Using our fact, faith, and function formula, this is where your faith in God's Word and promises needs to be exercised. Paul wrote concerning this process, "Likewise reckon ye also yourselves to be dead indeed unto sin, but alive unto God through Jesus Christ our Lord" (Romans 6:11).

Reckon is a bookkeeping term. It speaks of something that you can calculate and count on, something that is not a matter of feeling but of fact. You don't have to just close your eyes and pretend you are victorious in Christ. You don't have to clench your fists and grit your teeth trying harder to be victorious in Christ. You need to act in faith on what you know to be a fact. And the fact is that Christ died for you, and you died with Him. Now you must reckon on it.

Add Up the Facts and Make the Right Decision

You may ask, "How do I reckon?" If you're saved, you already know how to reckon because that's how you got saved. You believed the fact that Jesus Christ died for you on the cross, and you appropriated or took to yourself the forgiveness He offers and were freed from your sins.

You added up the facts the way a bookkeeper adds up entries in the ledger, and you concluded that if you would repent of your sins and receive Jesus into your heart, you would be saved. And you took that promise to the bank of heaven and cashed it, so to speak.

Now in the same way that you reckoned on your salvation, you must reckon on your sanctification and daily victory. You use the same process of spiritual accounting. I know that's so because the Bible says, "As ye have therefore received Christ Jesus the Lord, so walk ye in him" (Colossians 2:6). You didn't just feel or wish your way into salvation. You "crunched the numbers," to use a popular phrase, and came up with the fact that Jesus died for you. Your feelings about your salvation followed the fact of Christ's death, burial, and resurrection.

Suppose you sleep so hard one night that you can't believe it when your alarm goes off the next morning. You open your eyes and say to yourself, *It can't be morning already. It feels like I just went to bed.* But your alarm clock says it's morning, and when you open the blinds the sun is coming up. You stagger to the kitchen, and sure enough, the clocks on the coffeemaker and microwave say it's morning.

Now, your body and mind may be telling you it's still the middle of the night. But you would be foolish to go against every clock in the house and the earth's fixed rotation and crawl back under the covers. It doesn't matter how you feel. The fact is that it's morning, and you need to reckon on that by getting up.

You see, biblical reckoning involves making the right decision based on the facts you have. I love the story of the naive newlyweds who had never managed money before and weren't doing a very good job. One day they got a bill marked "Final Notice."

"At last!" they said cheerily as they threw the bill into the trash. "That takes care of that one. We won't be hearing from those people anymore."

That's not biblical reckoning. We're talking about making an accurate accounting of the facts and then making the right decision. I must reckon that the old Adrian is dead to his own plans, wishes, and will. And I must daily reckon that Jesus Christ is alive and well in me.

Put to Death Your Dead Old Man

Paul summed it up so well in Colossians 3:3-5: "For ye are dead, and your life is hid with Christ in God. When Christ, who is our life, shall appear, then shall ye also appear with him in glory. Mortify therefore your members which are upon the earth." Then he listed a "rogues' gallery" of the sins to which our flesh is prone.

"Mortify" means "to put to death." Now it may seem like doubletalk to say that your old person is dead, and then in the next breath to say that you need to put to death the old person and its practices.

But this is not doubletalk. What the Bible is saying is that we must reckon on what we know to be true. Paul was talking about appropriating what is already a fact. It would be like my dad saying to me as a boy, "Adrian, you're a Rogers. Now act like it." God is saying, "You're My child. Now act like it." The difference is that while earthly parents cannot empower their children to behave, we have the power of the indwelling Holy Spirit to help us live righteous, victorious lives.

The late, great preacher Dr. Stephen Olford, a beloved member of our church, said, "There is no demand that God places upon you that is not really a demand upon the Jesus Christ who lives in you." Jesus Christ is alive in you; you are alive with Him. You must reckon it to be true.

You Need to *Yield* Something to Enjoy Liberated Living

Remember our three words: *know, reckon,* and *yield.* We come now to that third power-packed word in Romans 6 that we need to understand in order to live in victory. Yielding is a function of our will. It deals not with identification or appropriation but with your emancipation. "Let not sin therefore reign in your mortal body, that ye should obey it in the lusts thereof. Neither yield ye your members as instruments of unrighteousness unto sin: but yield yourselves unto God, as those that are alive from the dead, and your members as instruments of righteousness unto God" (Romans 6:12-13).

Here's the thing. Jesus died for you, and His righteousness became yours—that is *imputed* righteousness. When you yield to Him, that is *imparted* and practical righteousness. It cannot be done without Him, and neither will He do it without you. You must do the yielding, and when you do that, God does the liberating.

Let's look at two other verses and then talk about what it means to yield to Christ and how to do it. "Know ye not, that to whom ye yield yourselves servants to obey, his servants ye are to whom ye obey; whether of sin unto death, or of obedience unto righteousness?" (Romans 6:16).

And again, "I speak after the manner of men because of the infirmity of your flesh: for as ye have yielded your members servants to uncleanness and to iniquity unto iniquity; even so now yield your members servants to righteousness unto holiness" (v. 19). What does it mean to yield?

You Must Dethrone Sin

First of all, there must be the dethronement of sin. "Let not sin therefore reign in your mortal body, that ye should obey it in the lusts thereof" (Romans 6:12). You don't have to let sin have its way. Don't let sin be on the throne of your life so that you obey it like the slave you no longer are.

You must understand that you have the authority to evict sin and its power from your life when you yield to what you know and reckon upon. You can choose whose servant you will be and what your life will produce. You can say to the devil when he comes with his enticements to sin, "Satan, you are a liar. I'm no longer your slave. The person I used to be is dead and buried with Christ, and I have resurrection-life. Therefore, you are an imposter and a pretender to the throne of my heart. You have no right or authority in my life, and I will no longer allow the members of my body to be your tools."

You have to evict Satan the same way you would an unwanted person in your home. A widow once allowed a man to move in with her on the premise that he would help pay her bills. The man convinced her they could just live together without marriage, and she foolishly allowed him to move in.

But then her conscience began to smite her. Not only that, but the man was obnoxious and rude and didn't pay his part of the bargain. So she told him, "I want you to move out."

But he said, "I'm not going anywhere. You invited me in here. I have a right to be here, and I'm not going to leave." The woman tried everything to make the man leave, but he refused. Finally she hired a lawyer, who went to the judge and got an order of eviction that said the man had to move out.

The woman took that court order back to her unwanted "houseguest" and said, "See this? It's a court order requiring you to leave. Either move out now and don't come back, or I'm going to call the police." So the man finally left.

You're going to have to do the same thing to Satan. You gave Satan a place in your life at one time. But that old arrangement is off because the person you used to be is dead, and you are a new person in Christ. So you can say to Satan, "I'm tired of this deal. I don't want you here anymore." And when he refuses to leave, take out God's "court order," His holy Word, and show the devil where God says he has no more authority over you. Satan cannot stand against the Word of God; he has to leave.

You Must Enthrone Christ

Now it's vital to dethrone sin and Satan, but that's not enough. You must also enthrone the Savior in your life. Again consider Romans 6:13, "Neither yield ye your members as instruments of unrighteousness unto sin: but yield yourselves unto God, as those that are alive from the dead, and your members as the instruments of righteousness unto God."

Another passage that helps us understand what it means to yield to Christ on a practical, everyday basis is Romans 12:1: "I beseech you therefore, brethren, by the mercies of God, that ye present your bodies a living sacrifice, holy, acceptable unto God, which is your reasonable service."

The word "present" here is the same Greek word as "yield" in Romans 6. It means to turn something over to another. You yield when you not only kick Satan off the throne of your life, but enthrone Jesus. The reason you need this second step is that nature abhors a vacuum. If you leave the throne of your life empty, the usurper will rush back in to take over again. Enthroning Christ means you have the right Person in control.

You Must Enslave Yourself to Jesus Christ

Now this one may throw you a little bit. But I use the word *enslave* purposefully, for that is exactly what Paul calls us to do if we would live victoriously. He twice used the word *servants*, which means "bond-slave," in Romans 6:17-18: "But God be thanked, that ye were the servants of sin, but ye have obeyed from the heart that form of doctrine which was delivered [to] you. Being then made free from sin, ye became the servants of righteousness."

You may be saying, "What's this about being a slave? I thought I was going to be free." No—at least not if you think being free means you don't have to answer to anybody. When you came to Jesus Christ, you traded your slavery to sin and the devil, which leads to destruction, for slavery to Jesus Christ, which leads to joy and eternal life. You are identified with Christ, and you are forever bound to Him as a bond-slave.

You may say, "I don't want enslavement." But being bound to Christ brings liberty. Let me tell you what you get when you become a slave of Jesus Christ.

First, you get *a new freedom*. Did you see it in verse 18? You have been "made free from sin." Jesus doesn't make us slaves against our will. That's the devil's game. When you yield yourself as a bond-slave to Christ, you discover what true freedom is. You serve Christ out of love, devotion, and gratitude.

Second, your freedom will produce *a new faithfulness*. "For as ye have yielded your members servants to uncleanness and to iniquity unto iniquity; even so now yield your members servants to righteousness unto holiness." We are talking about being righteous and holy in a very practical way in your everyday life.

And third, it follows as night follows day that if there's a new freedom and a new faithfulness, there will also be *a new fruitfulness* in your life. "But now being made free from sin, and become servants to God, ye have your fruit unto holiness" (v. 22).

Would you like to have a fruitful life? Then know that you have been crucified, buried, and resurrected with Christ to a new life. Reckon it to be so by appropriating resurrection power to live each day. Yield yourself to God and become a free bond-slave of Jesus Christ. Recognize the fact of your total identification with Christ. Put your faith in Him as you reckon on the basis of that fact. And begin to function as someone who knows and believes this.

The devil doesn't want you to understand any of this or act upon it. But now that you know it, ask God to help you to live each day in blessed victory. And He will!

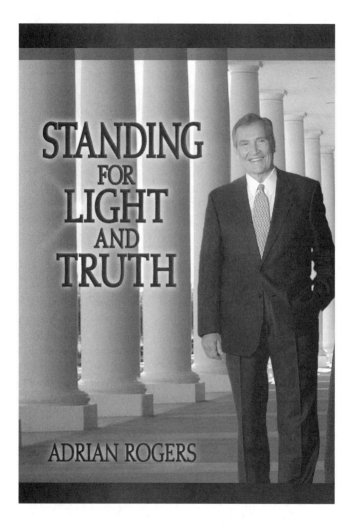

STANDING FOR LIGHT AND TRUTH

Adrian Rogers desires people to be brought from darkness into light
so that they can understand the truth of God's message through His
Son and through the Bible. Though salvation is the ultimate triumph
over evil in an individual's life, there are many battles to be fought and
won as we cast off the darkness of what life is without Christ. Here
is encouragement to continue to grow in conformity to Christ's light
and truth. Marked by Dr. Rogers's friendly style and graciousness,
these sermons highlight God's solution to the darkness of the world.

THE LORD IS MY SHEPHERD

The 23rd Psalm's beautiful lines feed and comfort our souls. But its greatest gift is that it offers what we all need—the secret to satisfaction in this life, and in the one to come—and promises what we can all experience—an intimate relationship with the loving Shepherd who fulfills the very longings of our souls. A tender look at each phrase of Psalm 23 shows how Jesus meets the deepest needs of every person. Accompanied by beautiful illustrations, Pastor Adrian Rogers's words direct those who long for true peace and satisfaction to the all-sufficient Good Shepherd.

THE POWER OF HIS PRESENCE

One of the Bible's most marvelous truths is that Christians are temples of the living God. This book is aimed at helping you integrate this grand truth into your life so you can start fully enjoying your true identity in Christ.

> "This book is a rich feast for the hungry soul. If Christians understood the profound truth that we are God's temple—His very dwelling-place—surely our lives would be different. Adrian Rogers has unfolded this truth with straightforward, practical, biblical wisdom."—John MacArthur